SUMMONING THE WHIRLWIND

For West Hill U.C.,

May these sermons
be a blessing to all my
spiritual friends at
West Hill U.C.

Peace,

Bruce.

Summoning
the
Whirlwind

Unconventional Sermons
for a Relevant Christian Faith

BRUCE SANGUIN

Canadian Memorial Press
Vancouver, BC
2005

Copyright © 2005 by Bruce Sanguin

Canadian Memorial Press
1825 W. 16th Avenue
Vancouver, BC
V6J 2M3
Phone (604) 731-3101
Fax (604) 731-5113
office@canadianmemorial.org

Library and Archives Canada Cataloguing in Publication

Sanguin, Bruce, 1955–
    Summoning the whirlwind: unconventional sermons for a relevant Christian faith / Bruce Sanguin; edited by Mark Haddock.

ISBN 0-9738098-0-9

    1. United Church of Canada—Sermons. 2. Sermons, Canadian (English)
I. Haddock, Mark, 1956– II. Title.

BX9882.S25 2005   252'.0792   C2005-902617-0

Cover Art Object: Chen Rong, Chinese, first half of the 13th century
Nine Dragons, (detail)
Chinese, Southern Song dynasty, dated 1244
Ink and touches of red on paper
46.3 x 1096.4 (181/4 x 431 5/8 in.)
Museum of Fine Arts, Boston
Francis Gardner Curtis Fund
17.169

Edited by Mark Haddock
Copy-edited by Carol Zhong
Design and layout by the Vancouver Desktop Publishing Centre
Printed in Canada by Ray Hignell Services Inc.

For Ann

Voice of the nova
Smile of the dew
All of our yearning
Only comes home to you
O love that fires the sun
keep me burning
—from *Lord of the Starfields,*
by Bruce Cockburn

Contents

Preface

In the spring of 2004, a number of us attending Canadian Memorial United Church in Vancouver independently arrived at the same conclusion: that the sermons of our minister, Bruce Sanguin, were too good to simply disappear after the 15 to 20 minutes during which he delivered them on Sunday mornings. We knew them to be well-crafted, thoughtful reflections on what it means to be a follower of the Christ, these 2,000 years after Jesus' life as a Jewish peasant and mystic. Carl Jung might speak of our collective conclusion as synchronicity, but in our desire to publish Bruce's sermons we were simply motivated by the desire to share the inspiration we had received with others. Recalling that Leonard Cohen marked his fiftieth year with the publication of *Book of Mercy*, which has one poem or meditation for each year of his life, we set out to celebrate Bruce's fiftieth year in a similar fashion.

The most difficult task in preparing this collection of sermons, not unexpectedly, was in selecting from the banquet table of options. I am very appreciative of assistance from several members of Canadian Memorial and Bruce's previous congregation at West Hill United in Ontario. The selection team included Ann Evans, Natalie Hall, Peggy Hall, Kay Metheral, Melinda Munro, Kirsten Nowack, Joan Smith, Glenda Thomson, Stephen Ward and Meguido Zola. After the sermons were collated, invaluable editing assistance was provided by Dorothy Buckland, Melinda Munro, Jeff Seaton and Glenda Thomson. Carol Zhong made an enormous volunteer contribution of her professional talents as the final copy editor.

Bruce's sermons are for those who aren't afraid of being challenged, whether it be intellectually, spiritually, or perhaps most difficult of all, in our rather comfortable lifestyles. His starting point is always the life and words of Jesus. But rather than isolating them, as you sometimes see on posters or coffee mugs, Bruce paints the religious, cultural and political context for Jesus' teachings by leading us through recent scholarship and biblical criticism. He distills Jesus' central truth, wisdom or life principles, and then applies it to our here-and-now. He draws connections for us where we might least expect them: perhaps the latest film, book, newspaper, rock song, scientific discovery or decision by political leadership. Bruce is always sensitive to and respectful of individual judgment and moral conviction, but also willing to take risks. Occasionally, he disturbs and prods our sensibilities but gets away with it because of his personal honesty, integrity and willingness to openly examine himself at the same time. We don't feel we are being "preached at" so much as guided through a mutual process of revelation and discovery.

Sermon-making has a long and healthy tradition, represented by writers as diverse as John Donne, Martin Luther King Jr., Barbara Brown Taylor and Fred Craddock, to name just a few. In the case of sermons that endure into literary form, there is a significant melding of the spoken and written word. Bruce's sermons are missives for our time that retain the casualness and conversational quality of public speech as well as the beauty and craft of a good essay. They are therefore not merely occasional pieces but public reflections worthy of reading and rereading. Like the whirlwind in the Book of Job, if entered into with an open and questioning heart, they will unsettle us, lift us out of our conventional ways of seeing the world, and surprise us with a new vision of wholeness beyond what we might have imagined.

—Mark Haddock

Introduction

At a pivotal moment in Jewish theology, some daring soul decided to challenge the conventional wisdom that God rewards the righteous and punishes the sinners. As well as being pervasive, it was also a tenacious belief, preserved in various forms even into the 21st century. The heated argument between Job and his well-meaning but unhelpful friends reflected a turbulence that always precedes new creation and the emergence of new meanings. This turbulence is symbolized in the story by the whirlwind out of which the Creator speaks.

The field of chaos theory has identified the vortex as a natural manifestation of balanced turbulence, the necessary condition for life and creativity. Much of what passes for the Christian faith is biased toward preservation of the "Truth." It lacks sufficient turbulence, the natural equivalent of uncertainty and doubt, to create the vortex out of which God creates a new heaven and new earth. In John's gospel, Jesus tells Nicodemus that the Spirit is like the wind, beyond our control. The most powerful sermons I've heard are not afraid of creating enough uncertainty for the sovereign Spirit to blow away our truths with a deeper truth.

On the cover of this book is a section of a painting called *Nine Dragons*, by Chen Rong, a 13th-century Chinese artist, which now hangs in the Museum of Fine Arts in Boston. It depicts dragons, symbols of creative power in China, emerging out of a whirling vortex. Spirals have long been associated with transformation. Two years ago, I dreamed that a tornado was fast approaching a bus in which I was traveling. When it hit, the bus flipped two or three times before it settled on its side. The passengers, including me, were frightened but unharmed. After climbing out of the bus,

I was approached by a man who told me that I had been selected to name a brand new species of tree. The tornado was the harbinger of a new creation. I knew I was about to undergo a profound change in my life.

The sermons that have been the most powerful for me seemed to aim for and emerge out of the whirlwind. After hearing such preaching, one has a sense that something like a tornado has touched down deep in one's soul, overturning old habits of thought, and outworn attitudes and beliefs. Bruce Cockburn writes, "The tide of love can leave your prizes scattered, but when you get to the bottom it's the only thing that matters." Such preaching can only happen when the preacher understands that his or her own life must reflect the balanced turbulence of the whirlwind. I want to know that the preacher's own life is vortex-shaped.

Jesus himself reflected this balanced turbulence. Out of the whirlwind that was his life, death, and resurrection a new creation, the Kingdom of God, was born.

He came to bring not peace but a sword, to redefine his family according to willingness to do God's will, and to non-violently shake up the arrogant assumptions of Empire and the patriarchal institutions of his day. Even Jesus' preference for telling parables was deliberate. John Crossan points out that, whereas mythology creates the world, parables dismantle the very mythology upon which worldviews are formed. They act like vortices. The listener is drawn inexorably toward the centre by the apparently innocuous narrative, only to discover that s/he has entered into a swirling force powerful enough to overturn and re-create.

To encounter this force in Jesus of Nazareth, the risen Christ, week after week, and to do this with authenticity, is to put oneself in the path of the whirlwind. Anything worth reading in these sermons is the direct result of trying by God's grace to be honest about that encounter over the years. Discipleship means being willing to risk the whirlwind. What is required is not so much adherence to a set of beliefs, as the courage of Job to withstand the pressures of conformity and risk an encounter with the living God who makes all things new.

The people in the congregations I have been privileged to serve—at Centennial-Rouge and West Hill in Scarborough, Ontario and Canadian Memorial in Vancouver, British Columbia—have been my partners in ministry, my friends, and my soul mates. These sermons emerged out of those relationships. They were written out of my deep affection and respect for them. Oftentimes it was the very sermons I was sure had gone too far, created too much theological or ecclesiological turbulence, that were most appreciated. We preachers tend to play it too safe and then use our congregation's assumed timidity as a cover for our own.

I owe an immense debt of gratitude to Mark Haddock, who put in countless hours editing sermons and managing the project. Most of the choices for inclusion were made by members of the congregations I served, working in teams. I am grateful to them for their wisdom and for taking the time to help with the project.

I want as well to thank the Very Reverend Dr. Bruce McLeod, who taught me homiletics in seminary and saw something in me I could not see in myself. He also is one of the finest preachers I have ever heard. Thanks as well to the Very Reverend Dr. Robert Smith, who summoned up a whirlwind every time I heard him preach.

I dedicate this work to my wife, Ann, who has witnessed each and every one of these sermons take shape, patiently listened to countless half-baked ideas, corrected me when I got my facts wrong, supported me when I questioned my calling, and challenged me when I didn't make any sense. Her own dynamic faith and unswerving love call forth the best in me.

Doubt, Our Faithful Companion

*But Thomas said, Unless I see the mark of the nails in his
hands, and put my finger in the mark of the nails and my hand
in his side, I will not believe.*

It's been a difficult couple of weeks to be a Christian. First,
Tom Harpur, an Anglican priest, theologian and journalist I
have a lot of time for, released his new book, *The Pagan Christ*. He
has influenced my own thinking throughout the years. So I was a
little taken aback to discover that he's come to the conclusion at
the end of a long and distinguished career that the whole Christian
story, along with Jesus himself, is fabrication. It's pieced together,
he claims, from ancient Egyptian and Mesopotamian myths. I've
heard the theory before, but it was more than a little disconcerting
to hear it coming from a man who, not so long ago, claimed to believe in the bodily resurrection of Christ.

Then, Doug Saunders, a columnist for *The Globe and Mail*, wrote
an article refuting the claim that Jesus was a social prophet concerned with the poor and with social justice. The title of the piece
was "Jesus, the Social Reformer: It Makes Nice Fiction." Using
historian E.P. Sanders to undermine the scholarly research of the
Jesus Scholars, especially John Crossan (who is also a mentor of
mine), he concludes his article claiming to speak for Albert
Schweitzer, the great medical missionary: "The real Jesus offers
nothing to people seeking a better world today." In one sweeping

article, Mr. Saunders writes off Jesus, the Jesus scholars, and John Crossan—all people that I admire. One can't help but wonder if he could get away with claiming that Moses or Mohammed have "nothing to offer." All this was coming at me as I was preparing my Easter sermon. I'm thinking about Jesus being raised from the dead at the same time as these two guys are putting him back in the grave.

In the face of such full frontal assaults, it is possible to start questioning one's own beliefs. Doubt can seep in. Maybe I'm crazy. Maybe everything I believe is an illusion. I mean I like hanging out with all these people on Sunday morning, but is it all true? How can we know? The story of doubting Thomas is written for you and me, the ones who were not privileged to touch the wounds of the risen Christ and yet who have "come to believe" at a time in history when such belief is held in suspicion or even derision by many. It is also meant to help those who are in the process of sorting out what exactly they do believe about Jesus and the story of his life, death, and resurrection.

I'm glad that there is a story of a doubter, because most of us, at some point in our faith journey, doubt what it is we're asked to believe, just as Thomas doubted the claims of his friends that Jesus appeared to them. He was holding out until it made sense to him personally.

Last Tuesday, our eco-spirituality group heard Brian Swimme talk about the secret of life emerging on earth. It is "balanced turbulence." It has to do with the balance between the gravitational force and the electromagnetic force. He gave the example of three planets, only one of which has come to life. Jupiter was so turbulent that it has never developed past the stage of being essentially gaseous. Mars, in contrast, lost its creativity to rigidity. It got as far as red boulders but couldn't get any further. It needed more turbulence.

Earth is the one planet that came to life because it found a middle way, a balanced turbulence.

I think that doubt is the spiritual equivalent of cosmic turbulence. If you have either too much of it or too little of it, your spiritual life will be stunted. Too much doubt and you can't commit to anything; you lack the conviction of your beliefs. Too little doubt and faith fossilizes into dogma; you begin to believe that you and your little group possess the absolute truth. When this happens, a healthy dose of doubt is just what the Divine Doctor ordered. Spiritual discernment involves knowing when it's time to open up to the turbulence of doubt and when to allow one's current beliefs to gel.

When I went into seminary, I was equipped with a knapsack full of rock-solid beliefs, red boulders as far the eye could see. I was a Martian. I was ready to take on those professors I'd been warned about, who would tempt me away from Jesus as my personal Lord and Saviour, who would try to convince me that the Bible wasn't the literal word of God. I'd been warned and I was ready to do battle. I was, to put it mildly, pretty hard to live with. I knew the truth. By the end of the first year, my belief system had gone 12 rounds with these professors and I had taken a beating. One particularly lovely professor, who has just recently passed away, Dr. Heinz Guenther, would end every class, looking directly at me, I was convinced, point to his head and say: "Think! Think!" I was filled with doubt, sure that the devil himself had gained a foothold in my soul. The low point was going to see the movie, *Being There*, with Peter Sellers playing the role of a simpleton gardener. For some reason, this simple man got the reputation of being somewhat of a spiritual genius. He would say something like, "spring follows winter, and summer follows spring," and everyone would be dazzled by his wisdom. As I watched, I became certain that this was exactly what everyone had done with Jesus: we turned a simple Jewish peasant into a Christ figure! It was all a hoax. I remember being in the Toronto subway system feeling disoriented and worried that I was having a breakdown. In one year, I had undergone space travel—from Mars to Jupiter.

But it's what I needed in order to get back to earth, back to a balanced turbulence in which faith can evolve and flower. This has happened many, many times in my faith journey. When you're going through a doubtful period, it can seem like an unwelcome visitor, even an enemy, but in the end it turns out to be a companion of faith. Every time, I emerged with a deepened commitment to Jesus and his way. It causes you to clarify what is essential to your faith and what is extraneous. It makes you go deeper, beyond platitudes and inherited beliefs.

The role of doubt ultimately may be to help us realize that this faith journey is not so much about believing the right things as it is about encountering Christ, crucified and raised. Thomas refused to believe what others told him. I think this is healthy, actually. And if we apply healthy doubt to the story of Jesus Christ, we also need to affirm that there is such a thing as healthy doubt towards books that we read and articles in *The Globe and Mail*. I've discovered that beliefs come and go, as we move through stages of life and life experiences. But the story of the doubting Thomas says that the Risen One came to him in the midst of his doubt, and that's ultimately what mattered. I'm not saying that Christ will appear to us the way he appeared to Thomas. But I am saying that he will appear to us, each in our own way, not only despite our doubt but possibly because of it.

I am saying that something happened to cause a bunch of frightened peasants to leave their hiding place and challenge the world with the good news of Jesus Christ. The author of John uses language that might seem strange to us: "He breathed on them and said to them 'Receive the Holy Spirit'." You see, just as God breathed upon creation in the beginning and gave it life, so now the Risen One breathed upon the disciples, initiating a new creation. They received power and grace, to forgive sins, to heal, to live non-violently, to build communities characterized by love and compassion and acceptance of all. When I need evidence that Christ is alive, all I need to do personally is to look out in the congregation any Sunday morning. I see healers, peacemakers, persons of enormous compassion, people passionate for justice. I see a community loving each other and yearning to share that love beyond the walls of this congregation. I do not exaggerate when I say this. I see people who have received the Holy Spirit and believe Jesus when he says: "Just as the Father has sent me, so I send you." This much is beyond question.

—April 18, 2004

Paying Homage: Persian Wisdom

ISAIAH 60:1-6; MATTHEW 2:1-12

*We observed the rising of his star, and we
have come to pay him homage.*

I want to talk about two distinctive religious pilgrimages this morning. One is ancient and the other is modern. The first is the ancient visit of Persian astrologers, the "wise men," to pay homage to the Christ child. The other is the modern pilgrimage of thousands of American Southern Baptists to the Biblical land of Persia, now known as Iraq, to convert the heathen Muslims. Both are well-meaning, spiritually motivated enterprises. But they represent two radically different models of faith and two different notions of how to get along with people who have a different faith from one's own.

The International Mission Board of Southern Baptists regards the current occupation of Iraq as a unique opportunity to win the souls of the Iraqi people for Christ. John Brady, the head of this organization, has sent an urgent appeal to the 16 million members of his church. Jerry Vines, former head of the Southern Baptist Convention, has described the prophet Mohammed as a "demon-possessed pedophile." Franklin Graham, Billy Graham's son, who delivered the invocation prayer at George Bush's presidential inauguration, has described Islam as a "very evil and wicked religion." Jon Hannah, a missionary who has recently returned from Iraq, having distributed 1.3 million Christian tracts, has concluded, "The Muslim religion is an antichrist religion."

They deliver food and clothing to the Iraqi people but, says this evangelist, these people need spiritual nourishment even more. That nourishment just happens to come in the form of the Southern Baptist belief system. This is one model of Christian mission and evangelism.

We have the Truth, capital T; their faith is nothing more than a lie, and therefore they must be undernourished. The primary purpose of being a Christian is to convert other people to our faith. The Muslim people quite naturally understand this for what it is, a holy war.

A different model is presented in Matthew's gospel this morning. The Magi notice "a star at its rising." The symbolism is important. Here we have wise people scouring the night skies, not for signs that they have the Truth but for signs of the truth wherever truth might choose to show itself. They have the wisdom to realize that the Holy One is not restricted to revealing Herself to only their people. They've taken their heads out of their own Bibles long enough to gaze up and out at what is the source of our fundamental unity, rather than what divides us. The wise ones intuited what science has now confirmed, that the basis of the unity of all peoples of faith is biospiritual. We have come from the same place and are made of the same stuff. We are stardust, reconfigured in human form, in-spired by the Creator. They gaze up at the stars and realize that a very special human being is about to be born, a child who is meant to transcend cultures, transcend religious differences, and point us all in the direction of a compassionate Father, the love which fired it all into being.

This star points them in the direction of Israel. They make the journey to Bethlehem in order to pay homage to the newborn King of the Jews. The poignancy of this story in light of the current mutual hatred between Iraq and Israel is not lost on us. Persia had a long history of kindness towards the Jews. When Cyrus of Persia conquered the Babylonian Empire, he allowed religious freedom to the Jews. Many returned home to Jerusalem to rebuild their Temple. The wise men inherited their wisdom from a culture of religious tolerance. Notice they go to Israel for a single purpose, to pay homage. They have no intent, or need, apparently, to import their religious beliefs. They open up their treasure chests and offer to the baby gifts of gold, frankincense, and myrrh. Not a mention of religious tracts.

Every Saturday morning, Ann and I go to Granville Island Market to get our groceries. When we've finished shopping, I end up at the Tea Store. There is a pleasant young man who works there. He told me that he was interested in theology and he was thinking of enrolling in a particular theological college, which made it clear that he was heading down a fundamentalist path. I told him that I would like to give him a book to read if he was interested. He became extremely cautious and said he'd have to run it by his pastor. I realized that what I wanted to do for him was to save him from my own experience of fundamentalist Christianity. In the end, I decided against giving him the book. I had been given too many books over the years by those who thought I was in the grips of the antichrist, if not the antichrist himself. And how would my gesture be any different from handing out tracts quoting John 3:16? It's time the religions of the world, including our own, got over having to convert everyone to their belief system. The Magi offer an alternative.

What would ecumenical relations with other faiths look like if they were homage-based? What would it mean for Christians to make the long journey across strange cultural and religious landscapes, bearing only gifts of respect for all that is sacred in other traditions? Just after the occupation of Iraq, people of this congregation visited Muslim mosques and worshiped with them. We invited Aziz Khaki, President of the Muslim Federation, to come and address our gathering at Peace in the City. The Rev. Dr. Barry Cooke is organizing an inter-faith event for this spring, which will feature persons from all faiths and of no particular faith, including the Dalai Lama of Tibet, Bishop Desmond Tutu, and Václav Havel. These are modern-day versions of the journey of the Magi. We need to be looking for and following the rising star of respect among different faiths.

It seems to me that we can learn from the Magi in another respect. Their wisdom extends to intuiting those people and political systems that are contrary to the very principles of life itself. In their encounter with Herod, they recognize a person and a political system that is anti-life. Herod embodies a paranoid worldview that is the enemy of all that is sacred. Where there is abundance, Herod sees scarcity. Where there is security, Herod sees imminent threat. Where there is love, Herod feels judgment. Where there exists the possibility of shared power and wealth, Herod uses his muscle to ensure a disproportionate amount falls his way. Where there is diversity, Herod imposes monocultures of his own creation. Where there is the threat of real democracy, Herod silences the people. Because of the Magi, the faiths of the world can withdraw allegiance from these systems and work together to articulate and enact an alternative vision.

As Christians, we express this vision in response to the revelation of Jesus Christ. We need to do this passionately and with all the conviction we can muster. We need to honour our sacred traditions, symbols, and narratives as sacramental; they have the power to open us up to the deep mysteries of God. The Magi were steeped deeply enough in their own tradition that they could make a pilgrimage into another culture and religion. They enjoyed the security of their own faith system sufficiently that they could pay homage to another. This, too, should be our model. I believe that the deeper we go into our own faith system, the closer we get to God, and the closer we get to God, the more we are informed by values of diversity, inclusivity, and respect for the inherent dignity of other people and faiths.

Notice that, after their encounter with the Christ child, the Magi "returned home by another road." We can take this as a metaphor suggesting that their encounter with the sacred centre of another religion had a transformative effect on them. Matthew doesn't say, mind you, that they converted to Christianity after meeting the baby. Many of us make that assumption. They were probably Zoroastrians. They were so when they arrived, and nothing in the story even hints that they became followers of Jesus afterwards. They went home. But they went home by a different road, meaning they allowed themselves to be influenced by the experience. The United Church has missionaries around the world. But they don't go to their placements with all the answers. If you want a picture of what that kind of arrogance results in, read Barbara Kingsolver's *The Poisonwood Bible*. You may remember that the missionary insisted on baptizing the African people in the river. They thought he must be crazy, for they knew what he hadn't taken the time to find out: the river was filled with crocodiles.

Sometime, ask our elders, Kay Metheral or Muriel Bamford, what it is like to follow a rising star across different religions and cultures. Each spent a good portion of her ministry in India. They went with a set of skills, in their cases as nurses, skills that had been requested by the people themselves. And I think they will tell you that they returned home by another road, profoundly affected by the experience, having received at least as much as they gave, and having found Christ in the people they served, whether they were Christian or Hindu. May the wisdom of the Magi prevail.

—*January 4, 2004*

Blessed are the Poor

I don't know if you were able to catch the documentary on CBC about the journalist who went to live for a month with an Ethiopian family. The plan was to live exactly as the family lived. The camera crew was instructed not to give him any food to eat while filming. The family of four farmed for a living. They received an allotment of grain every month, to supplement their food. The problem was that the amount of grain they received was enough for two days. After it ran out, they were forced to eat what they called wild cabbage. The journalist kept his commitment and ate only the cabbage, which he discovered was no more than a weed. After a week of this, he became weak. The weed gave him diarrhea and stomach pains. He assumed that, somehow, the Ethiopians had adapted to this food source because it's basically all they ate. Then he found out that they have exactly the same reaction to it, which left him dumbfounded. They never complained. After two weeks, he was desperately hungry. He couldn't fathom how the mother got up each morning and went into the fields to put in a full day of work. Where did she get the energy? While he was there, this Christian family was required by their church to fast for three days, if you can believe it, which they faithfully accomplished. At the end of four weeks, he had lost 40 pounds and was emotionally and physically spent.

I imagine that the crowd that came to listen to Jesus and be healed by him was similar to this Ethiopian family. They traveled miles, and what they were in search of as much as anything else was hope. They were hungry and they were poor and they were sick, and these conditions are intimately related. Jesus couldn't feed them because he himself lived from hand to mouth, trusting in the people of the towns and villages he visited to provide food and shelter. When we pray the prayer he taught us and we come to the line, "Give us this day our daily bread," we should be careful about elevating the phrase to the status of metaphor too quickly. Although daily bread can mean spiritual sustenance, to a hungry person living day-to-day it is, in the first place, a petition for food. Jesus, then, is preaching to the poor, and when he delivers what have become known as the Beatitudes, take note: he's speaking to his own disciples, as well as to the crowd.

"Jesus looked up at his disciples and said, 'Blessed are you who are poor.'" His first followers were counted among the poor.

As I read the Beatitudes, Jesus' compassion struck me hard. I don't know all of what he might mean by saying these strange blessings and curses. I say "strange," because those of us who are not poor have been taught to think that wealth is what constitutes the blessed life, not poverty. But statistics tell us that any accumulated wealth over and above that required to meet the basic requirements of shelter and food does not correlate with increased happiness. Material wealth, it seems, is not the secret of happiness.

But how can Jesus say that those who are poor are blessed? Jesus is speaking to those who probably don't have the basic requirements, so let's be sure we don't romanticize poverty. The Ethiopian family featured in the documentary is in a fight for life. There is little blessing in such conditions, as the documentarian discovered. When Jesus blesses the poor and the hungry, the joyless and the downtrodden, he is not in any way suggesting that these conditions are actually desirable. The happy, the satiated, and the rich like to imagine that there are implicit blessings in subsistence standards of living. We've all heard it before: "They have a simpler life. They have fewer worries. They have a joy we don't have." Well, it depends. If you're eating the same weeds and nothing else for three weeks, and living with diarrhea and stomach cramps, life is mostly misery, I suspect.

All I can think is that Jesus was giving them a word of hope. Only one who really knows hunger and poverty can stand before such people and offer hope and not offend. Here was a holy man standing before them, telling them that, if there is any justice in this world and the next, there will be a reversal of fortune, in which the hungry will be filled and those who haven't given the hungry a second thought in this life will have an opportunity to experience what they so glibly ignored. The laughter you have been robbed of in this life will be yours in the next. You will be honoured guests at the heavenly banquet. By this blessing, Jesus helps them to know that their hunger and their poverty were not natural, were not divinely ordained, and were not inevitable. Such was the thinking of the day. They deserved it. This kind of meritocracy in which the rich blame the lazy, unmotivated poor is persistent; it travels well across centuries. The possibility that hunger and poverty and sickness are the result of human beings colluding to perpetuate an entrenched economic system which privileges the few at the expense of the many never crosses some minds. "We are called upon to help the discouraged beggars in life's marketplace. But one day we must come to see that an edifice which produces beggars needs restructuring" (Martin Luther King Jr., *A Testament of Hope*).

According to scholar John Crossan, Jesus' commitment to living without money and without a store of food was an intentional strategy. He was modeling a return to radical dependency upon God and upon the community, an ancient economic system based on local economy. This was under siege by the new economic system introduced by Rome. This system was creating enormous wealth for the landowners and enormous poverty for those who were being forced to work for them. People were losing ancestral land because they couldn't afford to pay the taxes imposed by Rome. The fabric of an agrarian, local village system was being systematically undermined. By being forced off the land, they were becoming economically dependent on the rich, not on each other.

By going from village to village, literally showing up on people's doorsteps and being totally dependent on them for food and shelter, Jesus was attempting to repair and restore an economic system in which everyone had enough food to eat, in which wealth was broadly shared, and people took care of each other. It's the economic manifestation of the Kingdom of God.

Jesus knew that economics is at the heart of any discussion about the Kingdom of God. Economics is a spiritual matter. Here's a starting place for any discussion about the spirituality of economics. Shrink the earth's population to a village of 100 people:

- Six people would possess 59% of the entire world's wealth and all six would be North Americans.
- Eighty villagers would live in substandard housing.
- Seventy would be unable to read.
- Fifty would suffer from malnutrition.
- One would have college education.
- One would own a computer.

Our current economic system based upon self-interest can only take us so far. In 1776, Adam Smith penned his famous words: "It is not from the benevolences of the butcher, the brewer, and the baker that we expect our dinner, but from their regard for their own self-interest." At the time he wrote, Adam Smith assumed that self-interest would be moderated by responsibility to the community in which businesses operated. He never dreamed that the capitalist market system would morph into the rampant individualism of today. Globalization is nothing more than the spread of the ethic of individualism across the globe. Economics, simply defined, is "the division of scarce resources among competing uses and users." In our system, the division occurs through the market. There is an implicit assumption that the invisible hand of the market will distribute the wealth equitably. The invisible hand, however, favours those who, by virtue of birth, geographic proximity to natural resources, genetic predisposition, and technological sophistication, get a head start on the rest. These accumulate wealth at a disproportionate rate, as our village of 100 illustrates. This disparity became entrenched as the butcher and the baker morphed into an entity, the transnational corporation that Adam Smith could not have imagined.

Listen: corporations are neither bad nor good in or of themselves. But they, like all of us, are in need of redemption. The good news is that more and more enlightened presidents and CEOs are adopting a triple bottom line. They are putting people (fair labour practices) and the planet on an equal footing with profit. Self-interest is not a value that Jesus ever preached about, and it should not be the basis for a viable economy.

We have entered an ecological era, in which God is impressing upon the peoples of the earth that we already have an organic model that could serve as the basis of an economy that is both sustainable and just. That model is the earth itself. In this new era we need to be thinking from the perspective of the whole forward; what is good for the whole is good for the individual. When individual species take more than they need, the earth finds a way to reduce their numbers and restore balance. The intelligence of the earth, which reflects the intelligence of the Creator, will in the long run find a way to redress the imbalance we have created. The earth is self-sustaining precisely because it thinks of the needs of the whole. Either we follow its lead or we perish. We need an ecological economy. This is eco-logic. Our current system is based in ego-logic. Canadian Memorial has an opportunity to join a growing network of businesses and consumer organizations that promote, through responsible consumerism, a triple bottom line. It might be called the Conscious Consumer Network.

True wealth will be achieved when no family on earth has to live on weeds, when no species faces extinction because of our selfish pursuit of profit, and when we decide to live more simply in solidarity with the other species of the planet and the poor and hungry. This is the abundant life that Christ offers.

Today, when we come to the table, let's try and remember that this ritual of sharing the bread and the cup needs to be taken perhaps more literally than we have taken it before. We have such good hearts. If we ever happen to miss serving someone the bread and the cup in the congregation, there is enormous consternation. People wave their arms, point to the person who got left out, and afterward, we apologize profusely to the aggrieved individual. Some very good part of us understands that this ritual is a ritual of belonging, in which the bread is meant to be shared with all. Now can we imagine ourselves as a microcosm of whole? There is at least one Ethiopian family that has been left out. Can we imagine our consternation and deep concern extending beyond our congregation to the entire planet? We wave our arms and point in the direction of the 50 villagers who have been forgotten. I believe this is what our hearts are telling us. Blessed are those who are poor, for they will not be forgotten, not by us and not by God.

—*February 15, 2004*

Hockey Night In Canada, and the Myth of Violence

LUKE 13:1-9

He asked them, "Do you think that because these Galileans suffered in this way they were worse sinners than all other Galileans? No, I tell you; but unless you repent, you will all perish as they did."

I'm giving up NHL hockey for Lent. This might seem like a small gesture, I know, but we're talking here about someone who grew up watching Hockey Night In Canada every single Saturday evening with his family. It's the quintessential Canadian institution. I played hockey until the age of 15. I was the star player at seminary. I just happened to be the only one who could actually skate. So, when last night rolled around and my evening was clear, it took all the willpower I could muster not to tune in to the Canucks v. Senators game.

I was watching the hockey game on Monday evening between our own Vancouver Canucks and the Colorado Avalanches. When the score got to be 5–0 for Colorado, I knew that there was going to be trouble. Trouble came in the form of a vicious sucker punch by Todd Bertuzzi, rendering Steve Moore unconscious with two fractured vertebrae in his neck. It was sickening.

The reactions to the incident are fascinating. One acquaintance figured that the problem was with Steve Moore. If he had dropped the gloves when Brad May challenged him early in the game, it would have been all over. Mr. Moore broke two unwritten codes, I was informed. The first one was two weeks ago, when he showed no respect for Marcus Naslund, a league all-star with a late hit, and the second one was his refusal to respond to the challenge for a fight. The other reaction came from my next-door neighbour. I was out gardening when I heard Don Cherry's voice on his TV. I asked if I could come and listen. Technically, this didn't break my Lenten promise, as it was intermission. But I wanted to get Mr. Cherry's take. Well, I couldn't hear a thing because my neighbour was intent on trashing a *Vancouver Sun* columnist, Stephen Hume, for his scathing critique of the state of hockey. I happened to agree with Stephen Hume. I was dumbfounded when my neighbour called him a "sissy." That made me a sissy, too. I guess this makes Jesus a sissy. Jesus never dropped his gloves, as far as I know. Even when they sent Peter, the goon, out on the ice to protect him in the Garden, Jesus told him to put his stick down.

That unwritten code, which leads to the payback, didn't originate with the game of hockey. An eye for an eye and a tooth for a tooth was a law originally intended to limit violence. One could take an eye for an eye, but no more than this by way of retribution. The hope was that this would limit the contagious nature of violence itself. If my family killed one of your family members, you could kill a member of my family, but not the whole family. The problem that this code didn't take into account was the power of what René Girard calls "mimetic contagion." Once violence gets going, the participants start to imitate the violent behaviour of the others. You end up, in other words, with a bench-clearing brawl.

Violence is considered the fundamental and intractable problem in the Bible. By the sixth chapter of Genesis, God looks upon the human creation and laments at having ever created us. The problem, as

God saw it, was the violence in the hearts of human beings. God decides to start all over again and sends the Flood.

One of the fascinating insights of René Girard is his theory that only a victim lying in a pool of blood had the power to cause the violence to stop. Both sides stop fighting to gather around the corpse, overawed by the death but also by the power the death had to stop the violence. There is a "holy hush." Violence, embodied by this slain victim, had the power to end the greater violence, and it became institutionalized. It attained the status of sacred, because of its power to control greater violence. A Girardian analysis of the role of the hockey game in our culture is that it is the institutionalized, or culturally sanctioned, violence which we allow. Its purpose, albeit unconscious, is to act cathartically to control greater violence in the culture at large. Is this why there is such a pervasive resistance to eradicate fighting from the game?

Now, this is all theory and speculation. But I've got to tell you, watching the hockey game, I began to think that Girard was a genius. When Mr. Bertuzzi attacked Mr. Moore, the fans were on their feet cheering, all the players squared off with each other, the Canuck goalie stood at centre ice goading the opposing goalie to come and fight, and the commentators offered a blow by blow of who was getting the better of whom. Then the player went down in a heap, the blood started flowing out from under him, and then everything went silent. The players stopped punching each other and everyone gathered around the motionless body. A holy, sickening hush. I witnessed it right before my eyes. A wicked blow, a lifeless body, a pool of blood, the violence stops. Is something primal being played out here?

The problem, says Girard, is that we're at a time in history when the disgust and revulsion of experiencing a slain victim no longer has the power to deter further violence. Violence that is not cathartic is merely contagious. Two days later, the Canucks are playing Minnesota, and within the first three minutes of the hockey game, a fight breaks out. Saturday night, two minutes into the Toronto game, Tie Domi and another player are doing their best to hurt each other. God laments. Build the ark. Let it rain.

Jesus is listening in on a conversation in which people are trying to make sense of two events: some Galileans were murdered by Pilate in the midst of their religious sacrifices, and a tower fell on 18 others, killing all of them. The conclusion was reached that, in each case, these poor victims must have sinned to deserve that kind of fate. The corollary is that those reflecting on the incidents must be doing okay with God, because they've been spared. Jesus isn't buying it. Those who were killed by Pilate and by the tower were no worse offenders than the ones talking about it, he tells them. They are not relieved of the need to repent, simply because they were spared. In fact, unless they do repent, Jesus assures them that they will all similarly perish.

We like to be able to assign blame. It gives a certain order and predictability to the Universe. If we can find someone to blame, then the whole affair makes sense in light of his or her behaviour and we need look no further. The blame of the on-ice incident is the source of much discussion on the radio, TV, and in the newspapers. There is general agreement that Mr. Bertuzzi is ultimately responsible for his actions and deserves at least the suspension he has received. As mentioned, some think Mr. Moore himself played a role in the incident. Blaming the victim is usually reserved for women and the poor, so I was surprised to hear it emerge in this context. In typical fashion, Jesus shifts the attention back to where no one wants it shifted. Back on to the very ones assigning all the blame "out there." "Unless you repent," Jesus says, "a worse fate will befall you."

"Why? What did we have to do with it?" we protest. The incident occurred purely and simply within the context of a culture of violence, which is condoned and consciously promoted. The circle of complicity certainly begins with Mr. Bertuzzi, but from there it widens out like a net and covers all of us. It includes all players and the unspoken codes of violence that govern the game. Seventy NHL players are unable to perform right now, almost one in five suffering serious head, neck, and facial injuries. The circle then extends to the League itself and the owners of the teams. The National Hockey League takes its direction from the owners, who know that fights put bums in the seats. I imagine Mr. Bertuzzi sitting across from the League's commissioners, who gravely sit in judgment and mete out the sentence, sending a clear message that this kind of thing won't be tolerated. Well, it is tolerated, and encouraged. Referees are instructed to allow certain players to square off. Extending the circle of culpability we move to the TV networks and the commentators who call the fights blow by blow. CBC keeps Don Cherry in the Coach's Corner spot, as he defends the need for fighting. TSN was showing replays the next day of fights in other games, insisting that there is no correlation between fighting and Mr. Bertuzzi's behaviour. Next are the fans themselves. I've been at games in which one can palpably feel the crowd just waiting for the next fight and then cheering for the victor, especially if he's one of our own. We pay these kids millions of dollars a year to play gladiators on our behalf.

Finally, it is the myth of masculinity that sustains and perpetuates this culture of violence. This myth makes us believe that being able to withstand a little violence is one of the marks of manhood. Ann was asking me why I liked to watch *Mad Max* and yet became totally disinterested when she wants to watch *Terms of Endearment*. It's an oversimplification, to be sure, but it has something to do with feeling soft. We call them "chick flicks" and they make us feel soft. It's a term that is slightly derisory. We use it as men to leave no doubt that these kinds of movies belong to the women, not to us.

That soft feeling brings me dangerously close to the realm of sissy. Part of me wants to see fights in hockey games because it grounds me in my masculine identity. It gets my blood flowing. I feel hard. But another part of me never wants to see what I saw that night, ever again. In boycotting the NHL, I move over into this unfamiliar territory. What kind of a man boycotts hockey because it's too violent? The myth of masculinity gives me the answer: a "wuss," that's what kind of man. This myth keeps us from ourselves and keeps us from God. And it seems clear to me this myth is still driving the world toward destruction. Unless we repent, we will likewise perish.

We need to hear Jesus. None of us are relieved of the need to repent. We are so entrenched in this culture of violence that we see nothing wrong with allowing our teenaged boys to play the most violent videogames imaginable. New research shows that, although we may think it's just a game, when boys are hooked up to an MRI, it's clear that their brains react as though it were the real thing. Our children's brains are getting addicted to violence.

Mr. Bertuzzi is undeniably responsible for what happened, and he will suffer for the rest of is life for what he did to Mr. Moore. But in a very real sense, they are both victims of this culture of violence. Collectively, the human species still lives out of the myth of sacred violence, believing that violence itself is the solution to violence. Until we understand this and address this, Jesus' judgment is foreboding that we "will all perish just as they did."

Jesus tells a parable about a man who is fed up with a fig tree that is bearing no fruit. He tells his gardener to dig it up and burn it. But the gardener intervenes on behalf of the tree. He offers to dig around its roots, add some manure, and see if it can't bear fruit next year.

The man reminds us of the God in Genesis, who, in exasperation, concludes that human beings are a waste of space because of their violence. But God is also represented as the gardener who intervenes on behalf of the tree. Notice the gardener's intervention is to literally go to the root of the problem. I think of the gardener as Christ intervening on our behalf, asking God to give us another chance. Let's get beyond blame and, in solidarity with Todd Bertuzzi, make our confession of sin. "Lord, I love fights. They make my adrenaline flow. I want to see revenge meted out. I like movies about revenge." Let's get our own violence out on the table. For only with this kind of repentance can we begin the process of allowing God's gardener to get to the root of the problem, both within us and within our cherished institutions. We might learn a thing or two about being real men, by making our Lenten journey with Jesus to the cross. Dying with him may mean dying to our acceptance of violence.

—March 14, 2004

A Thief, a Kidnapper, and a Flood

ROMANS 13:11-14; MATTHEW 24:36-44

Now is the moment for you to wake from sleep.

Have you seen this offbeat HBO television series called *Six Feet Under*? It's about a family of morticians, the Fishers. Each episode begins with the death of some stranger who ends up figuring into the story line.

One episode, called "The Case of Rapture," centres on a 40-year-old woman named Dorothy Sheedy, a devoted member of the First Baptist Church. The story begins with two workers who are busy filling up inflatable sex dolls with helium, so that they can be used for a display at an adult film show. They load the inflated dolls into the back of their pickup truck. Preoccupied for a moment with an X-rated magazine, they stop, to avoid hitting a skateboarder. The sudden stop, however, loosens the net that is holding down the dolls. The dolls start floating upward toward the sky.

Coming from another direction, Sheedy is driving her car, with its "I Brake for the Rapture" bumper sticker. She's listening to a Christian radio broadcast on marital relations, uttering "Praise the Lord" in agreement with the host. Suddenly, she stops her car. She can hardly believe her eyes. Seeing the dolls floating way up above her towards the heavens, she mistakes them for actual human beings being lifted up. She concludes that it's the beginning of the foretold Rapture, when Christ removes all the right-believing

Christians from the earth, to spare them from the onslaught of the End of Days.

"Oh My Lord, Sweet Jesus!" Sheedy exclaims. She cannot contain her joy as a witness to the heavenly vanishing. Moving toward the imagined Rapture, her arms outstretched toward the clouds, she gets out of the car, walks into the road, and gets hit—and killed—by an oncoming car.

At the funeral home of the Fishers, her widower husband appears to fully accept the wife's death as the will of God. Clearly, her time had come.

Normally, I wouldn't touch the Rapture with a ten-foot pole. But when I was telling my daughter, Sarah, about the text that came up for me to preach on, and that I had absolutely no interest in the Rapture, she challenged me. "But Dad, it's in the Bible, right? So, it has to be meaningful, right? So, how can you just ignore it?" Out of the mouths of babes . . .

I think I did mention in a previous sermon that the most popular young adult fiction in the United States is a series called *Left Behind*. The "left behind" are the non-Christians who aren't taken in the rapture. Over 60 million copies of the books have been sold. The rapture is informing the consciousness of the next generation of Americans. Think about it. Sixty million kids are going to grow up expecting that, right in the midst of changing a diaper or making a presentation in the boardroom, or making love, they are going to disappear out of history.

Suffice it to say that the Rapture is not really on our theological agenda in the United Church of Canada. When Matthew's Jesus talks about two pairs of women working together and one from each pair gets "taken," I can't even pretend to know what it means. But I note with interest that nowhere in the text are the words "rapture" even used, only that they are "taken." You won't find it anywhere in the Bible, in fact. Reread Matthew: it sounds more like a kidnapping. It wasn't even used in Christendom until the Scofield Reference Bible, published in 1909, used the word in a heading and commented on it in the marginal notes. The Moody Bible Institute and other Bible schools spread the message, and spawned a whole rapture racket in which millions are being made.

The rapture is actually an old heresy, Manichaeism, which posits that the world is evil and the goal is to escape it. The message of Advent, however, is not about escaping the world. It's about getting ready to receive God, who is coming into the world and into our lives. Who knows when? Jesus didn't even know. He said, "about that day and hour no one knows, neither the angels of heaven nor the Son, but only the Father." So it behooves us, I would submit, to get our minds off the rapture and focus squarely on getting ready for the coming of Christ into our lives and our world.

We're a sleepy lot; that's what the Bible says in this morning's readings. "Now is the moment for you to wake from sleep," says St. Paul. And the Jesus of Matthew's gospel uses three images to get us to wake us from our slumber: a flood, a kidnapper and a thief. We have to prepare ourselves before it's too late.

We query why the coming of the Son of Man is associated with these very disturbing and somewhat frightening images. The Son of Man is a Jewish apocalyptic figure associated with God's victory over sin. Now, there are places in the Bible in which God makes a judgment about a sinful people and then acts forcefully to punish those who don't repent. That's why the frightening images. The coming of the Son of Man always has a component of judgment.

But I think it's more helpful to understand the coming of the Son of Man metaphorically. It's like the experience of being forewarned about an impending crisis, and having the choice either to ignore the warning and suffer the consequences, or wake up and make the changes necessary to avert disaster. God isn't the one who doles out the consequences; it's merely the result of our decision to ignore the warnings. One way or another, a life-changing, world-changing crisis and opportunity is announced. If we choose the way of ignorance, it's going to hit us like a flood or a thief in the night. The world as we know it, our lives as we know them, are about to be taken from us. Whether we see it as an opportunity, or it is thrust upon us as a crisis, is largely up to us.

So, one day you're driving to work and you feel this terrible pain running down your left arm. Your doctor had been telling you to lose some weight and stop smoking. The pain comes like a thief in the night, except that when you think about it, you knew you were a ticking time bomb. The coming of the Son of Man is a coming to consciousness, a heeding of the warnings or the facing of the consequences.

Your partner tells you "right out of the blue" that she's having an affair and wants a divorce. You're blind-sided, except that when you're honest with yourself, you can think of the exact moment five years ago when she hurt you and, rather than telling her, you shut your heart down and real intimacy ended.

I think of Roméo Dallaire crying out to the world from Rwanda that he was staring into the heart of darkness and if the world didn't intervene something terrible was going to happen. We woke up one morning in the Western world and 900,000 men, women, and children were dead; we slept through genocide. "For as in those days before the Flood, they were eating, drinking and marrying, and they knew nothing until the flood came and swept them all away." Except, of course, we chose slumber.

In his book, *A Short History of Progress*, Ronald Wright, who recently delivered the Massey Lectures, points out that every civilization in the past 5,000 years unintentionally destroyed itself. They were unable to see or unwilling to face the consequences of their commitments, their technologies, and their belief systems. Even as the signs were all around them for everyone to see, they refused to change their course. They chose to sleep through the destruction.

He tells of Easter Island, an island inhabited in the fifth century by migrants from the Gambiers. Over time, their population grew to 10,000. They split into clans and ranks: nobles, priests, and commoners. Each clan began to honour its ancestry with impressive stone images. Each generation of images grew bigger than the last, demanding more timber, rope, and human resources. Trees were cut faster than they could be grown. By 1400, there were no more trees on the island. The last tree was cut down, despite knowing that without trees they could no longer build boats or make roofs for their homes. Wars broke out over ancient planks. Yet, they continued to build the monuments, even when there was no wood to transport them into place. They built them at the site of the quarry, believing that the monuments were telling them that they would walk on their own after they were finished. Easter Island is now abandoned. Once a tropical garden teeming with wildlife, it is now a desert. The people killed off themselves and their land, blinded by what anthropologists call "ideological pathology."

The lesson of Easter Island is spelled out succinctly by Paul Bahn and John Flenley in their book, *Easter Island, Earth Island*. The islanders, they write,

carried out for us the experiment of permitting unrestricted population growth, profligate use of resources, destruction of the environment and boundless confidence in their religion to take care of the future. The result was an ecological disaster leading to a population crash . . . (eventually wars broke out over diminishing resources). Do we have to repeat the experiment of Easter Island on a grand scale? . . . Is the human personality always the same as that of the person who felled the last tree?

Leonard Cohen sings a wonderful, prophetic song called *Everybody Knows*. Everybody knows but chooses to ignore the signs. The Chinese word for crisis is made up of two characters: danger or hazard, and opportunity. God comes to us again and again, warning us through modern-day prophets, through friends and family, doctors and scientists, through alarming dreams at night. It's high time we opened our eyes before what's most precious to us is swept away, kidnapped, stolen from under us.

God's not going to come and lift us out of this world. God comes again and again to wake us up to the precious gift of life on this planet. God in Christ is the God of new beginnings and fresh starts. It's not too late to love this world we've been given, to love our lives as the God-given gifts that they are, to embrace this living jewel of a planet with all the love in our hearts.

—November 28, 2004

Does Not Wisdom Call?

PROVERBS 8:1-4, 22-31; LUKE 7:35

Wisdom is justified by all her children.

I t is interesting that, on Trinity Sunday, we are asked to reflect on a reading from Proverbs that features Divine Wisdom. Wisdom, translated from the Greek *Sophia*, is a feminine aspect of God. She pops into the Hebrew Scriptures unannounced in the Book of Proverbs, in the Wisdom of Solomon, in Ecclesiastes, and in other books of the Bible, making rather grand claims about her role in creation, in teaching human beings, even as Saviour of humanity.

To say the least, neither the Jewish nor the Christian hierarchies have quite known what to do with Her. It seems as though mainline Jewish theologians have identified her with the Torah, the first five books of the Bible and the associated laws. Christians don't quite know where She fits into our Trinitarian formulas; some say she is the Old Testament forerunner of the Holy Spirit. Some say she is the Holy Spirit, but then why do most Christians speak of the Holy Spirit as "he"? Paul occasionally speaks of the Christ as Sophia, but that didn't really take. In John's gospel, we are introduced to the *Logos*, the Word who was in the beginning with God. Is this Sophia? Could the Christ, who took up residence in Jesus of Nazareth, be feminine? Sophia is even spoken of as co-equal with God, not just as God's creative agent but also as the Creator Herself. This is why it's so ironic that She makes this appearance on Trinitarian Sunday. Do we just kind of fit her in to our existing Trinity by making her identical with Christ, the Spirit, or Creator? Or is she another dimension of divinity, in which case we would have a Quaternity Sunday rather than a Trinity Sunday? If you feel confused, don't worry. So are our scholars.

There is more than mere semantics at stake. At those points in church history in which communities have taken Wisdom seriously, it has had social consequences. Elaine Pagels points out that, in early Gnostic Christian communities, women were revered as prophets, teachers, and ordained as priests and bishops; they founded Gnostic churches. This never happened in orthodox churches, in which only male pronouns were used to describe God, Christ, and Holy Spirit. When the feminine is given sacred status, it has the effect of reshuffling our social, political, and religious systems to be represented by and function out of a feminine principle.

I can't tell you how many people have told me that I must read the novel, *The Da Vinci Code*, by Dan Brown. I am about halfway through the book and I must confess I do not like this style of writing. Any time someone has a point to make and decides to make it in the form of a novel, it always makes me wish the author would just write an essay and save me reading 400 pages. In any case, the point of the novel is that there has been a conspiracy against the feminine divine in the Roman Catholic Church. Mr. Brown makes the dubious claim that this is based in historical fact. Although I might not like this style of novel, it has struck a nerve in popular consciousness, bringing to light the indisputable fact that patriarchy and its privileging of a masculine worldview and systems of power has suppressed certain values and ways of being which have come to be associated with the feminine principle.

So who is this Sophia, who, despite patriarchy's concerted efforts, calls to us from every generation and perhaps most compellingly at this point in history? Elizabeth Johnson is one of the foremost scholars on Wisdom Literature. She summarizes her qualities:

> Sophia is a female personification of God's own being in creative and saving involvement with the world. The deeds attributed to her are almost identical with God's deeds. She fashions all that exists and pervades her creation with her pure and people-loving spirit. She is all knowing, all powerful, and present everywhere renewing all things. Active in creation, she also works in history to save her chosen people, guiding and protecting them through their struggles. She speaks with the authority of God, making the claim that listening to her will bring salvation while disobedience will bring destruction. She sends her servants to proclaim her invitation to communion . . .
>
> —Eleanor Rae, quoting Johnson, p.203, *Teilhard in the 21st Century*

Whereas the male God of Scripture, Yahweh, is often portrayed as a somewhat stern judge, exasperated with, and punishing of, human beings who don't toe the line, Sophia loves people. In our reading this morning, Sophia talks about herself as one who delights not only in God but in human beings. "I rejoiced before him always, rejoicing in his inhabited world and delighting in the human race." Sophia is the benevolent face of the divine, who has an attitude of childlike awe at the inhabited world and at the whole human race, a friendly Mother-like presence who delights in her offspring.

This portrayal of divinity presents a welcome corrective to the God many of us grew up with, I would hazard to guess. Many of us naturally tend to put ourselves under the judgment of God, measuring our behaviour, finding ourselves wanting, and interpreting bad luck as divine judgment. This stern image of God is the backdrop for the traditional presentation of Jesus as the sacrifice for our sins; only his blood sacrifice could possibly appease this Sunday School God who sees everything we do and knows everything we think. Sophia, in contrast, finds us delightful. It's not that we don't miss the mark from time to time, sometimes in a big way, but in Wisdom literature this is a result of ignorance, not inherent moral depravity. We are saved by overcoming our ignorance by incorporating the teachings of Wisdom into our daily lives, not by a blood sacrifice.

But notice it's not only "us" She finds delightful. "Us" is too often shorthand for our people, our race, those who believe the right things, as opposed to the non-believers, or the outsiders. Sophia's delight is universal. It's the whole inhabited world and the whole human race. The inhabited world includes all of life, human and more-than-human life forms. Far from being fallen, all of life for Sophia is divine revelation. In the Book of Job, it is an extended reflection on the wonder of creation itself that breaks Job out of the conventional understanding of his suffering as punishment. God's greatness is reflected in creation. Reintroducing Wisdom into the Christian tradition may provide the theological foundation for an ecologically based spiritual discipline of caring for earth. If the earth is divine revelation, then our debasement of it is debasement of Sophia; one could almost say the rape of Sophia. Sophia's love for the whole human race also breaks through that most pathological dimension of religions, that only those who believe as we believe are saved.

Where do we find Wisdom? She is everywhere. She speaks to us from the flowers, the mountains, the animals, and the developing Universe. But you'll also find her in the human realm "beside the way, at the crossroads, beside the gates in front of the town, at the entrance of the portals" (Proverbs 8:2-3). You'll find her, in other words, in the midst of the daily hubbub of life. All you have to do is notice your life in the midst of your daily comings and goings. Sophia is right here. What's tricky is to learn to hear her voice. Susan teaches a course in practical Wisdom called Centerpoint. The course simply and profoundly teaches you to listen to your own life. Autobiography, in other words, can be divine revelation.

You'll find Sophia "at the crossroads," at the intersection of different cultures, religions, and disciplines. Christians can hear Sophia calling from the Muslim mosques and Hindu temples. Last evening, I dropped in on an evening of Hindu chanting right here in the sanctuary. It was beautiful. It was a crossroads experience —different culture, different religion, and different language in a Christian church. Was that Sophia calling? I am hearing her voice currently where theology and science intersect. She calls to us to open, open, open to the diversity of life that passes by us every single day of our life. In other words, Revelation happens not just by opening the books of the Bible, or even exclusively through Jesus of Nazareth. Truth is certainly revealed through these, but it also comes to us in the deep, intentional, conscious reflection upon our own daily experiences. Whereas we have been taught that God speaks to us mainly from the past, through Scripture and through tradition, Wisdom tradition teaches that Sophia calls to us in the present moment of our daily life. Again, this shift from revelation as history and located only in certain people, to revelation as in the present moment and available in all creation, including our own lives, is a timely corrective.

In the reading from Luke's gospel, Jesus presents both himself and John the Baptist as children of Sophia. Many liberal scholars believe that of all the titles given to Jesus, Son of God, Son of Man, the Way, the Truth, the Life, this designation may originate with Jesus himself. In other words, the early followers of Jesus gave him the former titles, but child of Wisdom was Jesus' own preferred way of identifying himself. Both John and Jesus are messengers of divine Sophia, and indeed this makes a lot of sense if one examines the core teachings of Jesus. His parables are drawn from the daily life of his listeners, women sweeping, farmers sowing seeds, gardeners pruning, and people eating together. The point of his parables is in keeping with the message of Sophia: God's love is universal, encompassing all peoples, not just one's own people. God is more like a compassionate parent, who delights in and desires to give good things to his children, than a stern judge who metes out sentences. There is a narrow way, the spiritual path, which leads to life, and a broad way, the way of the money and power culture, which leads to destruction.

Wisdom has been calling to us throughout the centuries, it seems. She won't go away, even though we have chosen mostly to ignore her. She insinuates herself in subtle ways, so that even the men in charge of choosing the readings for Trinity Sunday end up choosing to include Her. As Jesus said, She is vindicated by her children, by those messengers who smile upon us with all Her delight and teach us Her ways of reverence for all living things, compassion, and justice for the poor.

—June 6, 2004

Sin Is Our Only Hope

MALACHI 3:1-4; LUKE 3:1-6

And he went into all the region about the Jordan, preaching a
baptism of repentance for the forgiveness of sins.

Once upon a time, an Inuit hunter went to see the local missionary who had been preaching in his village.

"I want to ask you something," the hunter said.

"What's that?" the missionary inquired.

"If I did not know about God and sin," the hunter said, "would
I go to hell?"

"No," the missionary said, "not if you did not know."

"Then why," asked the hunter, "did you tell me?"

Annie Dillard tells this story in her book *Pilgrim at Tinker Creek* to
point out that the church is guilty of being merchants of sin in order
to justify its existence. As the exclusive franchise holder of the tech-
nology of forgiveness, she detects a decided conflict of interest in
our investment in convicting the world of sin.

She has a point. I remember how my becoming a Christian required me to think long and hard about my depravity. The evangelist went to great lengths to convince me that, from the moment of
conception, I was a reprobate sinner. The corollary was that only
Jesus could save me from this condition. I couldn't get to heaven
without what this evangelist was selling. Well, that's one approach
to sin and I don't believe it any longer. We can't use it as a threat to
get people to buy what we're selling.

Christian preachers didn't invent sin. The story of Adam and Eve was written precisely because someone noticed that we're always screwing up. Most years in Advent, we light the candles of peace, hope, joy and love, usually because they seem beyond our capacity to realize, and we long for someone to show us how to manifest these qualities in our lives. We named sin as an aspect of Christian spirituality, which is helpful, yes helpful, in bringing us closer to God. The reality of sin in our lives is not a confirmation of our utter depravity. Rather, it acts as a signal that we've strayed from our original condition as beloved children of God, and that it is time to return.

I know some of you here this morning are familiar with the Enneagram, an ancient Sufi schematic that identifies different personality types. There are nine basic types with their own qualities and characteristics. For example, I'm a five, the Thinker. For a five to function in the healthiest way, I need to integrate qualities of the eight, the Leader. When I am most neurotic, I disintegrate to a one, the Perfectionist. There's nothing inherently better or worse about any of the types. But what I like about this ancient system is that it helps us to be aware of our regressive tendencies. I have a dark side and so does everyone in this congregation, and if you want to do your family, friends, and life partner a favour, get intimate with it. We should know when we're slipping into our disintegrated, most neurotic selves. When I start withdrawing into my head, and indulging a mood, it represents sin working in my life, and I'm responsible for doing something about it.

Advent is an opportunity to gain a deeper awareness of the ways in which we are responsible for being out of wholesome relationship with self, neighbour, earth, and God. We need to befriend sin, which, for the purposes of this sermon, are all those impulses and desires and social conditions that cause us to act out of our most disintegrated self, and in the process make our lives and those around us miserable. We sing *O Come, O Come Emmanuel* to express our yearning that Jesus will come into our lives to liberate us from the clutch of sin.

But here's the deal. In this Advent season, the only way to get to Jesus is to go through John, whom Walter Bruggemann called Checkpoint John. He was referring to that famous crossing, now gone, Checkpoint Charlie, between East Berlin and West Berlin, the alleged entry in to the freedom and well-being of "the West." In order to get there, you had to go through some rather rough and rude border guards; your papers had to be in order, the dogs would be sniffing around to make sure you were "clean," and you waited for what seemed an eternity for the green light, if you were lucky. Well, the only way to get to the Christmas Jesus is to go through Checkpoint John, for at least the next couple of weeks. His job description is found in the prophet Malachi:

> He's like refiner's fire and like fuller's soap; he will sit as a refiner and purifier of silver, and refine them all like gold and silver, until they present offerings to the Lord in righteousness.

John is the divine presence who holds our feet to the fire. He is the one with the fuller's soap. He's standing in the River Jordan and if we're intending to come anywhere near Jesus, we had better be prepared to be grabbed and immersed and washed clean before he's finished with us. He came to proclaim a baptism of repentance for the forgiveness of sins, but before we get to the forgiveness of Christ, there is the judgment of John. He is the one flashing the light in our eyes, asking to see our papers, making us sweat it out. All we want to do, we tell him, is to get to Bethlehem to see the little baby, maybe offer a gift. But he's telling us that the only gift the baby wants is a pure heart, because the baby's going to grow up and need us to be ambassadors, and the last thing he needs is a bunch of neurotics, talking about love and peace and joy, but fooling nobody.

Now, you might ask, where is John these days? We don't have to look too far. John can take the form of a close friend willing to give you a little honest feedback, or a life partner who has intimate knowledge of our most disintegrated self. My father sometimes plays the role of John the Baptist for me. While others are congratulating me for a fine sermon, he's holding my feet to the fire. "So tell me, Bruce, do you do what you just preached about?" This is what friends and family and lovers are for; I don't mean they're present in our lives to trash us, but rather to hold up a mirror in front of us so that we can take stock, maybe ask forgiveness, start anew. This is the tough side of love and we don't do our loved ones, or members of our congregation, any favours by tiptoeing around their bad behaviour.

In the film *Mystic River*, Jimmy commits a terrible crime, which his wife finds out about. In a scene in which he confesses what an awful thing he has done, his wife refuses to even hear the confession. Instead, she props him up. She tells him that he is a king, and that his children think he is a king and what good does it do any of them to be brought low by what he's done. Kings are forced to do terrible things for the people they are responsible for, and sometimes they make mistakes, but kings rise above it. In the course of her speech, you can sense his power return, his drooping shoulders straighten. Repentance is replaced by repression. The viewer is reminded of a prophetic line he spoke just before he enacted his terrible deed: "We bury our sins and wash them clean." Wrong, Jimmy. The gospel truth tells a different story. It is only when we bring our sins into the light of day that they may be cleansed.

When he and his wife choose to bury the sin, the promise of salvation is squandered by a conspiracy of silence. The violations and the violence of sin triumph. We can offer so much more to one another. I know a woman who began to resent how easily her husband hung out with the family dog. She noticed how he was always available to play with the dog, to speak kind and affectionate words to the dog, to touch him constantly, and tend to his every need. "Why," she wondered out loud one day in his presence, "don't you do that with me?" She is asking what is keeping them from loving one another more deeply, and so it is at core a question of sin. What would it be like if he could react non-defensively, with genuine interest and curiosity? It's an interesting question: why do I find it easier to love the dog than to love you? What am I afraid of? Is there anything you're doing to keep me away? It could be a Checkpoint John moment when they hold each other's feet to the fire, in love.

Sin is just part and parcel of the human condition. A lot of men I meet, and some women, seem to have the attitude that we were meant to be perfect, and anything less than perfection is shameful. The thing we seem to hate the most is the possibility that we're inadequate in any way; that we might not know something, that we're insensitive in certain areas, that we're selfish in some ways, that we have things to learn, and that who we are at times hurts others, by what we do and what we leave undone. But surely, when we're confronted by our incompleteness it's a sign that God's not finished with us yet. It's meant to be an opportunity for growth, not an occasion for either self-justification or its opposite, self-debasement. Psychologically, it's meant to be a signal pointing out those areas in our lives we need to work on. And theologically, when we're faced with that sin which is intransigent, which we can't seem to touch, it's intended to help us turn our hearts toward God for help. We shouldn't take sin so personally. It's God's way of helping us return from exile.

I'm not concerned by those who showed up at the River Jordan to hear John preach. There were soldiers, tax collectors, homemakers, and people from every walk of life, sinners every one, and they knew it. I'm more concerned about those who never show up because they refuse the holy judgment he offers and thereby refuse forgiveness and redemption. In the Hebrew Scriptures, the prophets had a direct line to the rulers, and they had a lot of power that they used. Moses gets an audience with the Pharaoh, Elijah goes to Ahab and tells him, "I'm on to you, sinner," Amos goes to the King of Israel and tells him if he doesn't turn his heart to the care of the widows and orphans, he's courting disaster. But today, prophets and poets can't seem to get anywhere near the kings and that should concern us all. The only time we hear confessions are times the kings are caught red-handed at the motel or behind the office desk or their mug shot is plastered on the front page for drunk driving. Otherwise, there's no Checkpoint John, no confession of sin and no growth in grace towards wholeness and toward God.

Ultimately, as Christians, we open ourselves to John the Baptist's scrutiny and repent of our sinfulness in order to make space for Christ in our lives. "All sins are attempts to fill voids," wrote the French philosopher Simone Weil. Because we cannot stand the God-shaped hole inside of us, we try stuffing it with all sorts of things, but it refuses to be filled. It rejects all substitutes. In the season of Advent, we learn that the God-shaped space is intended to be a womb for the Christ to grow and ultimately be birthed into this world. Through you. Through us. May it be so.

—*December 7, 2003*

Sin Is Our Only Hope is the title of a book by Barbara Brown Taylor.

Through the Eye of the Needle

MARK 10:17-22

"It is easier for a camel to go through the eye of a needle than for a rich man to enter the kingdom of God." The disciples asked, "Then who can be saved?"

Mary Jo Leddy tells a great story in her book *Radical Gratitude*. She works in a home in Toronto that provides shelter for refugee claimants. On one occasion, a young teenager from Africa came to stay at the home. Over a cup of coffee she looked out in the backyard and asked, "Who live there?" As far as Mary Jo could remember, there was no one camped in their backyard and told the young woman nobody lived there. But the young woman persisted. She pointed again, "Who live there?" Finally, Mary Jo realized she was pointing at the garage. For the first time in her life, Mary Jo actually "saw" the garage.

"IT. IS. A. HOUSE. FOR. A. CAR." Suddenly the garage stopped looking so normal to Mary Jo. Seeing it through the eyes of this young African triggered off a profound reflection on North American culture. What have we become, she pondered, that we have houses for cars, but not for people who live on the street? So, they went about trying to get a permit to convert the "house-for-a-car" into a "room-for-a-person." You won't be surprised, if you have had anything to do with zoning by-laws, that this proved to be impossible. One bureaucrat stared at her dumbfounded and said, "You can't do that, because if everybody did that then everyone would be turning their garages into rooms for people, and then there would be no room for the cars."

We live in a culture that cannot do without houses for cars. We have built highways for them to travel on; cities are constructed around the cars' needs and habits, countless thousands depend on them for their livelihoods. We are literally over-run, and run-over, by cars. Their ubiquity speaks to something far deeper than mere pragmatic need. The advertising industry has convinced us, with our cooperation, that we are what we drive. Cars make us sexy; with 300 horsepower under the hood they confer power; for the man enslaved to career and family responsibilities they represent freedom and liberation; for those who don't have time to pursue religious impulses, it's simply a matter of sliding into a Mystere, a Lumina, an Infiniti, or an Altima. Religious experience is only as far away as your new car. Do we own cars, or do cars own us?

Cars, trucks, SUVs won't simply get us from one place to another; they confer identity and status. We are even promised that they can deliver meaning and purpose to the owner. Along with leather seats, a new value system is a standard feature of this model. Now, take this promise and apply it to the thousands of brands of articles we possess and you have the basis for the sacred covenant we are all initiated into in our consumer culture. You buy this brand and it will deliver meaning, purpose, a value system, status, and personal identity. We are citizens of this culture whether we realize it or not, and even someone with the depth and integrity of Mary Jo Leddy is taken up in it. It takes a young woman who grew up in a completely different culture to reveal to her the absurdity of the status we have conferred upon a car. We build houses for them, for goodness' sake, and make laws to ensure that the house doesn't get used for people to live in.

The token that initiates us into the sacred covenant we make with consumer culture is money. It makes the world go around. Or rather, it makes this world go around. Because it is the token that gains us entrance into the sacred realm of consumer culture, it acquires a numinous, mystical quality. If we just have enough of it, we too can enjoy the happiness this realm promises. We can have the car and the house for the car, the holidays, the Versace jeans, the Gucci handbag, the new Titleist Driver which will make all the difference, the time-share in the Caribbean . . . or whatever it might be. Money is the magic token which can buy a life for us.

Let's be honest. We do get a hit from swiping the card and walking away with the latest product. For a few blessed hours, maybe even a few weeks, it is powerful medicine for depression or meaninglessness, but rarely longer than this, and we know it. It's not long before we're looking around at our lives, our eyes fixed predominantly, not on the car we bought last year but on the new model out this year, not on all those things which only recently conferred happiness but rather on all that we don't have. Dissatisfaction sets in. The system, in other words, is working as intended. Chronic dissatisfaction is carefully, consciously manufactured by the czars of consumerism. We trade our lives to get the money to get the things which promise entry into the world of instant status, identity, religious experience, and happiness, only to discover that the gnawing, chronic dissatisfaction we were trying to appease returns like fury. Then we repeat the process, hoping that this time it will be different.

John Paul Getty, the multibillionaire, was once asked how much more money he needed. His response was, "just a little more." This is the mantra of the culture we live and move and have our being in, and we are naïve to think we can escape it. Even our more noble spiritual yearnings can be understood as a symptom of chronic dissatisfaction. The next New Age book will hold the secret, just one more spiritual retreat, the next great workshop with the latest guru will deliver; "just a little more, and then we'll be satisfied." The truth is that the culture of consumerism can spill over and infiltrate every aspect of our being, so that the defining quality our 21st-century life is dissatisfaction. It begins with dissatisfaction with what I have, but ends with dissatisfaction with who I am.

So what? Isn't this just the way things are? Well, no, it's unnatural to be chronically dissatisfied. What is natural is the feeling that we will be attempting to evoke this weekend, sitting around with family and friends, over turkey and stuffing and wine. Gratitude. It is good that we set aside a day in the year to simply give thanks, to stop for one blessed day, and dwell not on what we don't have but on our blessings. What's not so great is how easily we'll set aside this soul-sanctifying day, and then on Tuesday re-enter the other world, as if it's the only game in town and we have no choice in the matter. In a culture of dissatisfaction, we're always moving on to the next thing, looking ahead to the next relationship, the next job; we're driven, driving ourselves towards the next thing that promises happiness. In our mad pursuit, we drive over the present, we flatten the abundance that is all around us, we crush the miracle of life as it is and whiz right by wonder. Gratitude is the first casualty of the culture of dissatisfaction.

Jesus invites us to enter into another realm, another world which no magical token, no amount of money can get you into. Why did the man approach Jesus in the story of Mark's gospel? He sought eternal life, but we don't know exactly what this meant to a first-century Jew. Perhaps he wanted to know that God was pleased with him and that his name was written in the Book of Life. What we do know is that he's dissatisfied with something, or he wouldn't be seeking the wisdom of a peasant rabbi. We are told he's a good man. Since he was a child, he has observed all the commandments. A good man dissatisfied, which, when you think about it, is not a bad description for many of us.

Jesus reads him like a book and tells the man who has everything, "You lack one thing." He's poking fun at the universe of the wealthy man, knowing in this world we're always just "one thing" away from bliss. You can practically see the man reaching for his wallet. Jesus takes one look at how he's dressed, how he carries himself, and knows that he's loaded. In one respect, the world this man inhabits is no different from the world we inhabit. If you lack one thing, then the natural question is: "How much?" Even in the world of first-century Judaism, your wealth enabled you to fulfill your Temple duties and keep the priests happy. Wealth gave you status in the religious community. That's why Mark says that the man is "shocked" when Jesus tells him to put his money back in his pocket. He had been taught that wealth was a sign of God's blessing. Apparently, he had never met a holy man whose eyes didn't light up when the wallet appeared (some things never change). And here's Jesus telling him that eternal life is not just another bauble you can buy. It's a quality of life that requires a passage through an opening in the heart so narrow that you can only make the journey by emptying all your pockets and emptying all your attachments to the false promises and false premises of this world.

For a rich man to get through this passage is like a camel squeezing through the eye of a needle. It's meant to be a joke, like a Cadillac squeezing through a revolving door, to use Fred Buechner's metaphor, but the disciples take it literally, as usual. It's like a kid who reaches into the cookie jar for a handful of cookies but can't get his hand out because he refuses to let go of a single cookie. Jesus is talking about being so attached to our possessions that they possess us. He's saying that, if one is still enchanted by the culture of money, by the life it promises to deliver, then the life this rich man was looking for, a life in God, is beyond reach, not because God denies rich people entrance (with God all things are possible) but because he won't let go. The spell money cast makes him doubt that there really is life on the other side of the needle, or even if there is, he's not willing to bet the farm on it.

The wealthy man walks away "for he had many riches." Note that the story says that Jesus loves this man who walked away. There is no condemnation, no judgment, just a deep understanding in Jesus of how powerful the cult and culture of money is. Who among us wasn't just a little fascinated by the $30-million Super 7 jackpot this past Friday?

It's a bit like a man traveling to the airport en route to be with his one true love. He gets to the metal detector and is asked not just to empty his pockets of change but to leave his credit cards, bank accounts and trust funds in the little tray. However, there's no guarantee he's going to get them back, in this story. To get to his loved one, he'll have to walk through the detector, which will sound an alarm if he tries to take any of it with him. Here's the thing—Jesus is the grand detector. If you want to enter the Kingdom of God, you've got to pass through him at some point.

If you choose love and take the step, you've shown that you have eyes to see and ears to hear, and in your heart of hearts you realize the life you've chosen is more real than the life you've left behind. The surprise just may be that there's a kind man on the other side who hands you back all your stuff, only now you know that's exactly what it is—stuff—no more, no less. It certainly doesn't define you, because now you know you're defined by love; it doesn't confer any status that means anything now, because being one who loves and is loved is what matters; it doesn't hold the secret to happiness, because you know that this stuff wouldn't mean a thing without love. The spell is broken, and now that it is, all these possessions might be useful after all in making the world a better place.

By the way, this world the rich man was invited to enter but could not, what he called "eternal life," and what Jesus called the Kingdom of God, is not so mysterious or otherworldly as we usually assume. The other side of the eye of the needle consists mostly of those gracious moments in life we miss on the way to something better. You walk outside to pick up the morning paper and the fresh air fills your lungs and you know there's nothing sweeter than that air that keeps you going, and it's making you think the Spirit itself is filling you up and giving you life; all you had to do was step outside. It's the moment when you passed by your partner on the way to brush your teeth in the morning and out of nowhere she's reaching for you and telling you she loves you, and the softness of her skin and of her gesture stops you and makes you catch your breath. It's the couple who've been married 50 years and counting, lighting candles every night and sharing one glass of wine with their evening meal. It's the smell of your baby's skin. It's lying out at night looking up at the stars when it finally breaks through to you that you've been given a free ride through this Universe on the planet earth, and it beats the heck out of any PNE ride. It's those moments when you realize there's nothing else to want, no place you'd rather be, you're complete and loved, and all that's asked for in response is what comes naturally anyway: simple, radical gratitude. And you start wondering what the world would be like if our economies and our politics were based not on dissatisfaction but on simple gratitude. The Kingdom of God begins with the awareness that you want to give your life to that possibility. And then you hear the voice of Jesus saying: "Come and follow me."

—October 12, 2003

If Ye Break Faith

MICAH 4:1-4

They shall beat their swords into plowshares, and their spears into pruning hooks; nation shall not lift up sword against nation, neither shall they learn war any more.

A member of this congregation, who is also a veteran of World War II, came to my office for a chat. He wanted me to know that he would be unable to attend this morning's service because he had to be at the cenotaph. He was a little upset that we chose to honour our veterans on the 11th rather than on Sunday, as has been our custom, because it meant other veterans couldn't be present. He understood this decision was taken because our 75th anniversary also fell on Sunday. I assured him that this wouldn't happen for another 25 years. But I could tell something wasn't right. As we continued to talk, the layers of concern were peeled back. He asked: "Well, who will lay the wreaths if our veterans aren't there?" I was taken aback by his question. I had simply assumed that any one of us could have laid the wreaths on their behalf. We talked about how, eventually, after all the veterans had died, it would have to be entrusted to those of us who didn't serve in the war. He had a solution. With two of his war friends he would underwrite the cost of a perpetual wreath, which would be on display at every worship service throughout the year. At the moment the Bible was placed on the table, a floodlight would shine on the wreath. Now, I'm not sure what we'll do with his proposal, but I began to wonder what was really going on in our meeting.

One way of understanding our conversation is that he was worried that our commitment to veterans was flagging. Could we be trusted to remember in the future? Does someone who didn't serve in war have the credentials to lay the wreath after the veterans were dead and gone? I understood these concerns. I have never been asked to risk my life in war, nor have I heard shells exploding near by. I've not seen a friend wounded or killed in battle. How could I possibly possess the empathy worthy of laying a wreath for those who gave their lives? However, there will come a day in the not too distant future when this task will have to be entrusted to the likes of me and to others who don't have first-hand experience. What was at stake here was captured in the last stanza of John McCrae's famous 1915 poem, *In Flanders Fields*:

Take up our quarrel with the foe:
To you from failing hands we throw
The torch; be yours to hold it high.
If ye break faith with us who die
We shall not sleep, though poppies grow
In Flanders fields.

In the Prince Edward Island window of our church, the story of David and three of his valiant soldiers from the Book of Samuel is captured in stained glass. A war-weary David and his army are encamped outside of Bethlehem, which is occupied by the Philistine army. He sighs, "O for a drink of water from the well at Bethlehem." Upon hearing this, the three soldiers break through the ranks of the enemy army and return with a cup of water. David takes the cup of water and pours it on the ground and utters the words inscribed on the window: "Is this not the blood of the men who went in jeopardy of their lives?" Colonel Fallis, who founded this church and chose the themes for the windows, says this is intended to signify "the moral obligation imposed on us by the sacrifice of others."

Certainly after World War I there was general agreement that memorials, and wreath laying, and remembering were not sufficient to fulfill our moral obligation. We were obliged to build a better nation by a recommitment to the moral ideals the soldiers died for. Don Seaton pulled out of the archives the first sermon ever preached in this sanctuary. The Reverend Dr. W. H. Smith, Principal of Church History at Union College in Vancouver, delivered the sermon from this pulpit, ten years to the day after Armistice, November 11, 1928.

"The coming of the golden age will be characterized by lofty moral standards of living."

He advocated a return to the true spirituality of Christ as the only way we could attain these standards. Then he went into a lament that was common after both world wars:

"Society today is convulsed on account of shocking immoralities, tragedies, lawlessness, broken homes, and barbarous inhumanities on every hand."

This sentiment was broadly shared after World War I. There was deep sadness that the sacrifice of the soldiers appeared to be for naught, as the unity of the nation during the war years deteriorated rapidly afterward. The disillusionment the average citizen felt was captured in a poem read at the dedication of the memorial in Priceville, Ontario, in 1921:

We thought to catch the torch ye threw,
And to the charge ye left, be true;
But once strife of arms was past
Then high resolves were overcast
With selfish greed. And lust to gain
Has put to flight the sweet, sad pain
Of sacrifice. And in its train
Went noble deeds. Are ye aghast?

We owe those whose lives were cut short in war and in peacekeeping missions the debt of moral transformation. But after 100 million war dead in the last century alone, we have to realize that war does not have the power to effect this transformation. It is a transformation realized only by a commitment to opening ourselves, individually and collectively, to a spiritual discipline of study, prayer, and being vigilant in watching the horizon for warning signs of escalating violence which could lead to war. We take up the torch by refusing to passively acquiesce to political agendas and strategies that have the potential of igniting global tensions.

King David's action of pouring out the water after his men risked their lives to get it for him is ambiguous. I think it can also represent the moral obligation, not just of ordinary citizens but also of our political and religious leaders. I cannot help but think that David abused his position of authority in this story. As king and as God's representative, he has a responsibility to ensure that the cause for which he is asking his men to risk their lives is noble. His frivolous articulation of a yearning for a drink of water is the moral equivalent of kings and popes throughout history asking men to give their lives for such ethically dubious causes as religious and political imperialism. Is it possible that his pouring out of the water is a gesture of repentance?

The direction of the current US administration is in my opinion breaking faith with those who died in previous wars. September 11th provided them with the pretext they were looking for to implement a geo-political strategy of using their unrivalled power to re-make the world in their own image. Some would say that image is democratic freedom; others would say it's in the image of G.O.D., gold, oil, and dominance. For the purposes of this sermon, I will give them the benefit of the doubt and assume that their goal is worldwide democracy. Although the goal of world democracy is a legitimate way of "taking up the torch," the present means of securing this goal will meet with resistance in the form of escalating terrorism.

The US has reversed decades of military doctrine and adopted a national security policy that includes the use of pre-emptive attacks against foes—real or perceived. The vast majority of the Muslim world perceives the occupation of Iraq as a declaration of Holy War, and in unguarded moments the US administration reinforces this perception.

As long as the US is perceived as waging a holy war against Islam, the average Muslim will support fundamentalist leaders. Furthermore, the nuclear arms race appears to be back on, as Russia has begun its own program of nuclear rearmament in response to the dramatic US commitment to finance their military dominance. Finally, in what way is the weaponization of space keeping faith with the 100 million who died in wars last century? As a church, we need to call upon the current US administration to pour out the water of their ambition upon the earth, for the sake of their young soldiers who are being sacrificed daily for a dubious cause.

I want to end with one more quote from Dr. Smith. In the context of identifying all the positive movements for peace which emerged out of the war, he mentions one that I could not believe he included. I can only imagine that he took considerable criticism for daring to speak it out loud. Remember, he is speaking to a sanctuary packed with dignitaries, filled with those statespersons who underwrote the cost of the stained glass; seated here were the widows and the sons and daughters of those who were killed on the battlefield. After mentioning an initiative to reach out to former enemies (The Alliance for Promoting International Goodwill), he writes:

> The most recent movement is that among the clergymen of Europe and Britain to the effect that they will no longer support war. They claim that war is so terrible it is better to endure evil than to commit it. It reminds one of Alexander Whyte's position: "It is better that evil should grow than that love should die."

The moral obligation we owe to those who have died in war is nothing less than fulfilling the ancient prophet's vision of a warless world, in which nation shall not lift up sword against nation and they shall study war no more. How we achieve it is open to debate, but perhaps it's time to allow this position back into the debate; after all, it does sound an awful lot like Jesus of Nazareth, to whom we owe our primary allegiance.

—November 11, 2003

Mary, Revolutionary Mom

LUKE 1:39-55

God has brought the powerful down from their thrones and lifted up the lowly.

I'm thinking about revolutions. I woke up in the middle of the night and realized that I'd missed all the big revolutions. I experienced a kind of yearning for the meaning of being part of something so significant. This didn't come out of the blue. I've been reading Jonathan Schell's *The Unconquerable People* and the history of the collapse of Soviet power in Poland and Czechoslovakia. But, if truth be known, it was Mary's song, the Magnificat, which caused me to pick up Schell's book after it had been sitting on my bedside table since last Christmas. "God has brought the powerful down from their thrones and lifted up the lowly." Revolutionary lyrics, I'd say.

Mahatma Gandhi came up with a revolutionary concept. Instead of blaming the British for the oppression of Indian people, he placed the responsibility squarely on the Indians themselves. He went so far as to say that the British imperial rule was completely a creation of the Indian people. This might seem like an earlier version of neo-conservative poor bashing. But Gandhi wasn't so much criticizing his own people as providing the foundation for their resistance to British rule. If the people created British rule, it follows that they have the power to uncreate them.

I believe and everybody must grant that no Government can exist for a single moment without the cooperation of the people, willing or forced, and if people withdraw their cooperation in every detail the Government will come to a standstill . . . The causes that gave the English India enable them to retain it. Some English say that they took and they hold Indians by the sword. Both these statements are wrong. The sword is entirely useless for holding India. We entirely keep them.

He so deeply believed in the power of non-violent non-cooperation to uncreate the powers that, once he committed himself to this mission, in his mind it was just a matter of time before the English left India.

Jonathan Schell describes the four great revolutions of modern history: the Bloodless Revolution of 1688 when King James fell to William of Orange, signaling a new chapter in British rule; the American Revolution of 1776; the French Revolution in 1789; and the Russian Revolution in 1917. Schell makes a compelling case that in each instance the revolution was over before it started. Once the people had withdrawn their allegiance, the ruling powers were already disenfranchised.

To give just one example, when the American people had had enough of an arrogant British Empire thinking that they should manage the affairs of the world (the irony is not lost on any of us), they simply stopped cooperating with the Empire. When John Adams found out that Major General Wilkinson was penning a history of the revolution, Adams lamented that the general would focus only on the battlefield. But Adams claimed the revolution was over before the war began.

The revolution was in the minds of the people, in the union of the colonies. The war? That was no part of it; it was only an effect and consequence of it; the revolution occurred from 1760 to 1775 before a drop of blood was shed.

The people withdrew cooperation and began to meet together to imagine alternatives. It made me think about church as one of these subversive meetings, during which we gather together to imagine a better world.

Now normally we don't think of Mary, the mother of Jesus, as a revolutionary. She is usually portrayed dressed in royal robes as if she is a member of the ruling class preparing Jesus to take the throne, I suppose. Nothing could be further from the truth. The Magnificat, Mary's song, which we heard today, is subversive. Notice how she uses the past tense to articulate her excitement:

> God has scattered the proud in the thoughts of their hearts.
> God has brought down the powerful from their thrones
> and lifted up the lowly;
> he has filled the hungry with good things,
> and sent the rich empty away.

Mary and Elizabeth have one of those subversive meetings. They're thinking it's already happened. She's pregnant with God's future, and the meaning she makes of this is that it might as well already have happened. She's taking the angel at his word. She says to herself, "Start the revolution with me."

Her cousin, Elizabeth, knew that Mary's capacity to believe it was part of the deal. "Blessed is she who believed that there would be a fulfillment of what was spoken to her by the Lord." This is a theme, by the way, in Luke's gospel that part of the revolution of the Christ event involved women having a voice and a central part to play in the manifestation known as Jesus Christ. In Mary's day, women had no voice. They were not considered valid witnesses in a court of law; they were virtually powerless. Luke knows what he's doing when he has this extended encounter between Elizabeth and Mary; it's a feminine conspiracy, a sign of the new age, like the conspiracy of Shiprah and Puah and the Pharaoh's daughter, who colluded to liberate the Hebrew slaves. It's as if Luke understood that part of what the birth of Christ was unleashing was a new feminine consciousness that would have an enormous effect on manifesting what had already occurred when Christ was born. It is interesting to think about the past 2,000 years as the slow unfolding of the revolutionary meeting between Mary and Elizabeth.

The last 2,000 years have seen the radical awakening of human consciousness to what Mary expressed in her song: that the world should be organized around the needs of the lowly, not the desires of the privileged. All the revolutions I've mentioned, including the Cold War, have been about this in one way or another. Even though we are witnessing in our era a shift toward a neo-conservative ideology, those who espouse and enact this agenda are required to justify their actions as being in the best interests of the poor. Some believe it. Some don't. But the fact that they feel like they need to justify their agenda according to the needs of the poor is new in the history of humanity. As René Girard points out in his writings, prioritizing the voice of the victim is a distinctively Christian development.

Some prefer to spiritualize Mary's song, claiming that, when she sings of the powerful on their thrones and the lowly, she is referring to our personal arrogance or humility. I don't doubt that her song addresses both the political and the personal, but we are wrong if we assume that it excludes the political dimension. The hungry that are to be filled with good things are Mary's neighbours who wonder where the next meal is coming from; more than once she has discretely left a casserole and a loaf of bread on their doorstep; Mary is intimately acquainted with these lowly ones, who've had to give up their ancestral land to pay taxes to support the rich and famous lifestyles of the ruling class. The rich who are sent away empty are the foreign landowners who hire the former owners of the land to work for subsistence wages. Mary's song has personal application but it is thoroughly political.

If it's true that the great revolutions of our time occurred in the first place in the hearts and minds of the people, then think what this birth of God in Jesus Christ means. This gospel revolution occurred first in the heart and mind of God. Could it be that the birth of the Christ is God's non-violent, non-cooperation with systems motivated by greed, ambition and power? Could it be that, in Christ, God was declaring that this kind of rule is fundamentally against the principles and ethics of the Universe? These eternal ethics are located in this Jesus of Nazareth, a nobody in the eyes of the world, but the very power of God if you believe the Gospel story.

That revolution announced by Mary, and named by Jesus as the Kingdom of God, has already come in Jesus. History then is the patient, non-coercive unfolding of God's intentions. It follows that our task is to not to create the Kingdom of God on earth. Tyrants, religious fanatics, overreaching Empires, and ideologues of every stripe have tried to do this for years, and still are doing it, with disastrous results. It's not up to us. God's already done it. Our task is to cooperate with God's vision manifest in Jesus Christ, and to withdraw cooperation from those powers that are not manifesting God's intentions. This is not a violent revolution we're called to, but a revolution of the mind and heart, which will manifest politically.

Let me end by giving just one example of this revolutionary, non-violent, holy cooperation, which necessarily is also non-cooperation with other powers. Some of you will remember Aiden Enns and Karen Schlitchting. They worshiped with us for a couple of years, and just recently moved back to Winnipeg. Concerned about the commercialism of the season, and the cost to the earth of this unbridled consumerism, Aiden organized a choir that goes to the malls to sing renditions of popular Christmas tunes. Only they've changed the lyrics substantially. As a result they are getting thrown out of the malls. Here's a verse of *Rudolph, the Red-Nosed Reindeer*.

Uh, oh, we're in the red dear
On our credit card it shows,
Christmas is almost over
But the debit line still grows
Shopping like Santa's zombies
Sent our budget down in flames
But all our Christmas spirit
Helped the giant retail chains.

Revolutionary lyrics, I'd say.

—December 21, 2003

Heavenly Citizenship:
An Earthly Perspective

PHILIPPIANS 3:7-4:1; LUKE 13:31-35

*But our commonwealth is in heaven, and
from it we await a Savior, the Lord Jesus
Christ.*

Secure in the knowledge that you were all well taken care of
last week, I was able to engage fully in a very powerful conference in San Francisco. This morning I would like to share with
you a little bit of what I bring home from the conference. As many
of you know, one of my abiding intellectual passions has been the
confluence of science and spirituality, particularly in the new cosmology. By "cosmology" I mean a worldview that is expressed in
narrative form telling the story of where we came from, where we
are going, and suggesting as well the purpose for our lives. By
"new" I mean that particular narrative of the developing Universe
given to us by science over these past few decades. It is new relative to the cosmologies of the classical religions, including Christianity, which did not have the benefit of modern science. Jesus, as
a man of his age, would have imagined the Universe to be three
tiered: the heavens above the dome of the sky, the earth sitting on
four enormous pillars, and a shady lower level under the earth,
called Sheol. It is the convergence of his spiritual sensibility that
this Universe is loving and compassionate and the scientific story
of creation that together brings us closer to the heart of Reality.

The new cosmology tells the story of a Universe flaring into existence 13.9 billion years ago, undergoing a series of massive expansions and contractions, the miraculous emergence of matter because of infinitesimal asymmetry between matter and antimatter, and matter winning out. As the Universe cooled, galaxies formed, stars imploded and exploded, releasing all the elements that now make up our bodies. One of these explosions resulted in our solar system. The sun is five billion years old, and not long after, earth emerges. Over vast amounts of time, earth figures out through plants how to transform the sun's light into food, and the great story of evolution on earth begins. When humans emerge a mere two million years ago, they are the result of all the plants and animals that came before. The amazing thing is that it's all made of the same stuff that came flaring forth out of the fireball. We share a biological kinship with every created being on earth and throughout the Universe. The stars are our ancestors. The primal people's intuition that the wolves and the turtles are kin is based on scientifically verifiable data. With the advent of the human being, consciousness was introduced into the Universe. We are the first generation of human beings to use this consciousness to become aware of the story of the Universe.

Then, in 1992, at a mega conference called the Earth Summit, two of these human beings, Maurice Strong and Michael Gorbachev, came up with the idea of creating an Earth Charter. One of our leaders, Dr. Mary-Evelyn Tucker, was intimately involved in the shaping of this Charter over the last 12 years. This Charter is the most comprehensive ethical statement for the human species ever created. After 13.9 billion years of evolution, it captures our most exalted vision of what it means to be a fully functional human community. It is the most negotiated document in history. Literally thousands of people—representing theologians of every faith, philosophers, politicians, and poets—weighed in on the process of giving it shape. It is the first such statement which assumes as its fundamental context the planet Earth and the evolving scientific story of the Universe. In the preamble, the Charter states, "Humanity is part of a vast evolving Universe . . . . Earth, our home, is alive with a unique community of life." The document implicitly acknowledges that even human rights need to be contextualized by the rights of the planet. It's like the instructions a flight attendant gives before take-off: "In the event of an emergency, if you're traveling with small children and the pressure drops, administer oxygen to yourself first, then to your children." Just as children cannot survive on a plane if their caretaker does not have oxygen, so if the earth loses the capacity to nourish us, if the biosphere loses its capacity to protect, if the air we breathe is polluted, we cannot adequately care for anyone. The earth's well-being is the bottom line for economics, politics, and social policy.

Listen to the headings of the Charter: Respect and Care for the Community of Life, Ecological Integrity, Social and Economic Justice, Democracy, Non-violence and Peace. Since coming to Canadian Memorial, I've been looking for a working definition of peace, because peace is our distinctive mission in this congregation. I think we've found it in this document. After 13.9 billion years of evolution, God is getting through to us, in and through conscious awareness, that what unites all religions, philosophies, and races is our common identity as offspring of a living, nourishing planet, and that the planet itself is a child of a developing Universe. God is getting through to us that we are at a turning point in the history of this story and that the continuation of life itself must be our common ethical foundation.

The essence of the conference in San Francisco was that our primary purpose at this point in the story of the developing Universe is to ensure the continuation of life. Not my life, not my religion, not my philosophy, not my ethnic identity, but life itself. Do you want to know where we are, existentially, at this point in history? This is where we've arrived. Do you wonder what we need to be about? This is our mission. Take a little chunk out of this Earth Charter, and give a little piece of your life to making it happen, and you'll discover profound meaning and purpose.

What we're about is ensuring that this great biospiritual adventure of the Universe, called the planet earth, continues. We are at the point where we cannot take this for granted. We need to be about cultivating a cosmological, planetary consciousness. We need to reinitiate ourselves into the life systems of the planet, and overcome the illusion of separateness. We came away from the conference with an urgency, in religious language, a calling. As Christians, we would say that the Cosmic Christ, as Creator and immanent presence, is now, like never before in the history of humanity, activating the minds and hearts of the human species

When Paul says in his letter to the Philippians that our "citizenship is in heaven," I don't claim to know all of what he meant. But I do know that he's making a point about intimate belonging. He intuits that we don't belong to the culture of those who are fixated with "earthly things." He means by this worldly values. He's referring to those who inhabit the planet from within an old ethic; "their end is destruction; their god is their belly, their glory is their shame." This ethic belongs to an age that we are collectively exiting at this point in history. Our economic, political, and social institutions, as well as our personal identities have been forged in a profoundly narcissistic worldview. This has resulted in the kind of irony Paul describes. The "glory" of the Western world, defined as success, wealth, our luxurious lifestyles, our plundering of the earth's resources is actually "shameful" when viewed from a heavenly citizenship. Susan DuMoulin has just returned from Guatemala, which she'll be telling you more about. But when you look at the "glory" of our lifestyles from the perspective of Guatemalans, living in squalor, you begin to appreciate the shamefulness of this glory. "Heavenly citizenship" is a cosmological, planetary identity and perspective.

We are entering a new age, an ecological age. Paul gets a glimpse of this new citizenship, and speaks of the expectation of the Saviour, the Lord Jesus Christ. Today, we might talk about yearning for a Christ consciousness, or the Cosmic Christ. Paul says that the Christ will "transform the body of our humiliation that it may be conformed to the body of his glory." From where I stand, I can't help but relate this transformation to the earth itself. The "body" which is humiliated at this point in history is the body of the earth. Because we are the earth in human form, we, too, inhabit humiliated bodies. The rivers, the forests, the oceans, the atmosphere, are in a state of humiliation; the spotted owl is humiliated by the destruction of its habitat here in BC. Our own bodies are humiliated by all manner of cancer and illness caused by the degradation of the earth. Indigenous peoples of the earth are humiliated. Half of the world's population is humiliated by a system that is just not working. The glorious body of the Cosmic Christ is a healed and renewed earth. As earth is renewed, our own bodies are renewed. There is only unity.

And let's not be naïve; if Jesus, as incarnate Cosmic Christ, is the mother hen who births us into a new age and gathers us under her wing, there are plenty of foxes intent upon ridding the world of such foolish notions. There are Herods in the political, economic, social and religious institutions for which the humiliation of most of the rest of the world and the planet itself is a small price to pay for their own glorious dominance. These resistant institutions and personalities are the ones Paul calls "the enemies of the cross." That is, they resist the suffering implicit in the transformation that is underway. They continue to violate social, ethical, and planetary laws because they refuse to die to the old to make room for the new. They refuse to imitate the way of the Christ. We refuse to imitate the way of the Christ, and follow him to the cross. This is the Lenten journey.

Jesus' own humiliation on the cross is a powerful symbol of God in Jesus taking this humiliation into God's own being for the purpose of transformation. This profound act of identification, this compassionate suffering with all of creation, is redemptive. We are called to go with him into this painful identification.

The resurrection of the Christ is the beginning of a transformation in which all of creation is given hope that collectively the wounded humiliated body of the earth will be transformed into the glorious body of the Christ. This will only occur as we are initiated into the sacred mystery, the glorious revelation of the earth as the body of God. This planet is the paradise God has given us. The time has come; God's time has come, to treat it as such.

—*March 7, 2004*

The Patient Redemption
of Violence

LUKE 22:14-23, 53

"But this is your moment, the hour when darkness reigns."

I suspect that more people around the world have opened themselves to the Passion of Christ this year than ever before. Mel Gibson's *The Passion of the Christ* has drawn a lot of people who otherwise wouldn't have bothered. That's not necessarily a good thing. On a previous Sunday, I preached about my concerns regarding the film. By providing no context, it runs the risk of perpetuating anti-Semitism. As well, there are a lot of strange scenes in the film you won't find anywhere in the gospel accounts. The reason is that it's inspired not only by the gospels but also by the visions of a nun, Ann Catherine Emmerich, who lived in the late 18th century. In her book *The Dolorous Passion of Christ*, she describes visions she had of Jesus' crucifixion. The book is filled with virulently anti-Semitic statements. It is this woman who inspires Mr. Gibson's understanding and depiction of the Passion. I want to talk briefly about the theology that underlies the film this morning, and then present an alternative way of thinking about Jesus' death.

Driving Mr. Gibson's portrayal of the Passion is a theological misconception that only the unimaginable suffering of Christ can atone for unconscionable sin of humans. Mr. Gibson learned well his catechism that taught him the Christ suffered and died for the sins of humanity. So he made a film that focuses exclusively on the suffering of Christ. It's almost as if his suffering saves us. Not his teaching, not his compassion or non-violence, and not his resurrection. The greater the suffering, the more effective our salvation. It's a compelling notion, especially for those who have committed sins for which they have not been able to forgive themselves. But the idea falters under scrutiny.

It suggests that God's best solution to the problem of sin is to knowingly send his Son to earth to be tortured and executed. It turns the same God whom Jesus taught was compassionate and loving into a child abuser and a murderer. In this theology, God sent his Son to be the innocent scapegoat to take our place, for our sin is so great that we deserved death ourselves. But Jesus pays the price on our behalf. Those who weep while watching the film are typically the same ones who have been taught that they deserved to be the ones being scourged and executed, but just look at what Jesus has done for them.

Now, if you believe this, then it's easy to really roll around in Christ's suffering. Each drop of blood flowing from his head is for me, each piece of flesh torn from his back should have been my flesh; you get the idea. This is the belief that generated Mel Gibson's movie. The film's intent is to get us to understand that this suffering was on our behalf, and that we therefore owe our very lives to him.

Besides what this belief does to our image of God, as mentioned, there are many other problems with it. I'll mention just one. First, Jesus had a way of dealing with sin, when he was alive. He forgave it. "Go and sin no more. Your sins are forgiven," he said over and over again to those he healed. Every Sunday we pray the prayer he taught his disciples to pray, "Forgive us our sins as we forgive those who sin against us." Not only did he believe we had the power to forgive sins; he insisted that we do just that as the key to a non-violent way of life. Jesus forgave sins and told his disciples to do likewise before he himself was crucified. Forgiveness of sin does not require his execution.

So how are we supposed to make meaning of his suffering and death as Christians? Well, I need to confess that, over the course of my life as a Christian, it's meant different things to me at different stages of my faith life. But this morning I want to talk about this event at its most basic level. I remember reading a book by Susan Sontag, *Illness as Metaphor*, about her struggle with cancer. She began to resent people talking about cancer as a metaphor. For example, we might talk about a "cancerous belief" or something "growing like a cancer." She protested that, as long as people were living with and dying of the disease, it shouldn't be used as a metaphor for anything other than what it is. It was offensive to her. Turning it into a metaphor diminished its primary and immediate meaning.

Right now in my Christian journey I feel the same way about Jesus' death. I've used the cross as a metaphor myself. Paul also uses it as a metaphor in the Bible. For example, he says that we need to be crucified with Christ in order that we might be raised with Christ. I understand this use and I'll probably use it again in my preaching. But at this moment in my own formation, I find myself taking the story at face value.

An innocent man is tortured and executed by the State and by a religious élite. It is an unjust execution of an innocent man for political reasons. If we must use it as metaphor, then it is a story of the violence in the heart of humanity. What gives it particular poignancy for Christians is that we believe that this man was the embodiment of the divine, and so it represents the violent rejection, not only of a good man but also of a God-man. We have not progressed very far when it comes to our violent natures.

It's the tenth anniversary of the Rwandan genocide, in which close to 800,000 Tutsis were brutally executed by Hutus. I was reading a story in *The Globe and Mail* about a Tutsi woman, Athanasie Mukarwego, whose husband was tortured and killed, and then she was raped repeatedly by busloads of Hutus over a 90-day period. They stood over her and told her they killed her husband by machete but she would die of rape, for inevitably she would be infected with AIDS.

As I read her story, I realized I was reading a modern passion story. At one point in her ordeal she was left alone with her three children, and all she could think of was using that time to kill them, so they would not have to go through what she was going through. As she made her way to the living room, she fell to her knees and begged God, "I doubted your existence. You set for me to be tortured. You know how I have suffered. Grant me the courage to be able to take the lives of my own children." And then, she said, "I heard a voice, saying, 'patience, patience'."

Athanasie survived and so did her children. She now lives next door to the men who raped her, and their wives, who did nothing. Every day she passes them, memories passing through her mind like a horror movie, unable to be shut off. The miracle is that she has found a reason to live, to work, to support other victims of rape. This, she says, is her therapy. She says that she must forgive those who did this to her and to her sisters and all the children. She must do it, she says, to break the cycle for her own children. The words from the cross echo from another tortured victim, "Father, forgive them."

This violence is not restricted to Rwanda, Sudan, Kosovo, or the Middle East. It's likely genetic, says researcher Dr. Tremblay. Having researched violence for over 20 years, he concludes that we are never more violent than when we are around the age of two and a half. Fortunately, he concludes, at this age children can do little damage. But, he warns, if we do not intervene intentionally to help our little ones learn to manage their aggression and reward them for acting generously and compassionately, we will end up paying later. In other words, teach them to be peacemakers, and teach them early.

The church's contribution to this education is to teach our children the way of non-violence, known in and through Jesus Christ. We tell this story of Christ's passion, year after year, to help us remember the depths of the violent impulse in human beings. But we tell it remembering that violence is not the end of the story. According to the earliest witnesses, God acted to raise Jesus up from the grave, as God acted to raise Athanasie from her own grave. We go into Holy Week confident that God will continue to act to surprise us with hope that we can learn a new way to be together as human beings. We hear a voice coming from the cross, "Patience, patience."

—April 4, 2004

Put to the Test

GENESIS 22:1-14

The time came when God put Abraham to the test.

This story of Abraham's willingness to sacrifice his son, Isaac, is both gripping and disturbing. I'd rather not preach on it, to be perfectly honest, but saying nothing about it may be worse than silence. As it stands, God puts Abraham to the test. God is wondering if Abraham has the stuff to be a leader of a great nation. The primary virtue required for the position is obedience. Now, obedience definitely has a place in the lexicon of virtues. But the question this story raises is: obedience at what cost? God asks Abraham to slay his own son by the knife as a sacrificial offering and as a sign of his obedience.

In my mind, this has parallels to military boot camp. One of the primary goals of boot camp is to establish the authority of superior officers to such an extent that, under pressure, the recruit will obey the orders of a superior. That is fine until a soldier is put in the position of being ordered to do something that he regards as inhumane. This is the position Abraham finds himself in; only the order is coming from God, as he understands God.

Do you remember the scientific experiment designed to test the limits of compliance in ordinary human beings to authority? A group of people was given instructions to reward correct answers and punish wrong answers of people in another room, whom they couldn't see. The punishment for wrong answers, they were told, was a mild electric shock. Of course, there were no people giving answers, but there were actors paid to respond audibly to the electric shocks. When the experimental group administered a shock for a wrong answer, they heard some screaming in the next room. The researchers assured them that it wasn't all that painful, and that if the experiment were to be a success, they would have to continue. The experimental group continued administering these shocks, despite the escalating blood-curdling screams they assumed were coming from real people. Their readiness to comply with an authority with relatively little incentive proved to be chillingly high.

So one of the problems I have with making the point of this story Abraham's profound obedience is how it renders both of the primary players. God comes off as a jealous five-star general testing his recruits' capacity for obedience. This God only relents when Abraham's spirit is broken and he is truly prepared to sacrifice his son.

Abraham, far from being a paragon of faith, in my view comes across as a rather pathetic pleaser, concerned more with pleasing a Superior than about following his natural instincts. This leaves aside, for the moment, the third player, Isaac, who no doubt lived with post-traumatic stress syndrome for the rest of his life, trying to reconcile his love for his father with the knowledge that his father would slice and dice him in a heartbeat if that's what God really wanted. And finally, there's the ram, caught bleating in a thicket, which becomes the acceptable sacrifice.

It gets worse. I was just reading in the *Christian Century* a piece by a modern theologian who was valiantly trying to redeem this traditional interpretation by drawing out the implications for Christian theology. Human beings are disobedient and sinful. God is divine Judge and therefore must render the punishment of death. But God intervenes. Once again God provides a ram caught in the thicket; Jesus, his beloved Son.

God, in Christ, becomes the acceptable sacrifice, paying the price for our sin. There are many problems with us, not least of which is that the brutal execution of the flesh and blood person, known as Jesus of Nazareth, is made out to be God's will. To believe this is to accept that God required human sacrifice as a modus operandi. I believe that Jesus' self-donation was inspired by God, not required by God, and this self-donation, which ended on a cross, wasn't for our sin but because of it.

So, let me tell you how I am currently making sense of this story. I'm thinking that Abraham heard two sets of voices. The first voice was the voice of the dominant religious and social culture of his day. As we know, this voice is often confused with the divine voice. The social and religious culture in Galileo's day heard God's voice telling them that the sun revolved around the earth. The same voice said that witches should be burned along with non-Christians. Christian slave-owners were sure they heard God sanctioning slavery. Up until relatively recently, there was general consensus that God agreed that women should be subservient to men. You can add your own examples.

The religious and social culture of Abraham's day required that the first-born son be sacrificed as an offering to God. Abraham heard this voice as the voice of God and was prepared to obey it. But even as the kindling was being loaded on the donkey, and the knife was being sharpened, the true voice of God was trying to break through. When asked by his son, "Father, where is the sacrifice?" Abraham tells him that God will provide the sacrifice. This is the point at which Abraham is actually challenging the voice of the status quo; he can't believe a true God would require him to go through with it. Only after raising his knife to slay his son does the true voice of God break through the religious and social norms. Abraham hears the voice of God telling him to substitute an animal for his son, and what happens in this moment is nothing less than the spiritual evolution of humanity. Abraham realizes that the true God is not pleased by human sacrifice.

This story marks the turning point in human consciousness, revealing that the spilling of blood is no longer seen as pleasing to or required by God. Later, the prophets, including Jesus, realize that even animal sacrifices were abhorrent to this God. This emerging image of God replaces a bloodthirsty Judge with a more compassionate God. The dominant theology of the cross, which interprets Jesus' death as a sacrifice required by God, is a giant step back in spiritual evolution.

So, we can affirm that God was indeed testing Abraham in this story, but it was a test, not so much about Abraham's capacity for blind obedience. Rather, it was a test to determine whether Abraham had the capacity to distinguish the true voice of God from the dominant religious and cultural voice of his day. This capacity for discernment, and the willingness to act upon the more authentic voice, is the mark of true spiritual leadership. Abraham passed the test.

This is a test for all of us. Those who struggle with addiction will tell you that the voice of the addiction is an authority that demands absolute allegiance. They will also tell you that, until they learn to distinguish between the voice of their addiction—a demanding, brutal god—and the true voice of God who provides an alternative to destroying all that you love, they are doomed.

There is another voice in our culture that is assuming god-like proportions. It is the voice of the market, sounded by those who see human beings and the earth's resources through an exclusively economic lens. It is the voice of economic globalization, which is asking us to define the human enterprise primarily as an economic one. The Market will save us, the Market is all-knowing, the Market is all-powerful and must be left to sort things out on its own without any government controls. Of course, there will be sacrifices. Two-thirds of the world will end up as a cheap labour pool; the earth itself becomes little more than a commodity, raw resources for the Marketplace; the short-term interests of shareholders take precedence over long-term sustainability, secure jobs, and service to the community.

Don't get me wrong. I am invested in the market; corporate profit is not a bad thing, but without any spiritual sensibility or holistic vision of the human enterprise, Market forces become just another word for Rampant Greed. It is this greed now that holds a knife over all that is precious and sacred. Our humanity depends on hearing and obeying an alternative voice.

With Abraham, we are being put to the test. Will we be able to discern the voice of the one True God that leads to deeper humanity from the false gods that lead to death and destruction?

—June 30, 2002

The Divine Strategy
for a New World

ISAIAH 42:1-9; ACTS 10:34-43

"Behold, the former things have come to pass, and new things I now declare; before they spring forth I tell you of them."

Leo Tolstoy, the great Russian novelist, tells a sad tale about how he decided that he would start things off on the right foot with the woman he was about to marry. In order to have a clean slate to start the marriage, he would be completely honest with her and let her read his diary. These diaries contained the lurid details of his sexual dalliances with other women before he met his fiancée. It backfired.

Sonya did marry Tolstoy but could never forget what she had read. "When he kisses me I'm always thinking, 'I'm not the first woman'," she wrote in her own diary. Some of his adolescent flings she could forgive, but not his affair with Axinya, a peasant woman who continued to work on the Tolstoy estate.

"One of these days I shall kill myself with jealousy," Sonya wrote after seeing the peasant woman's three-year-old son, who was the spitting image of her husband. "If I could kill him and create a new person exactly the same as he is now, I would do so happily."

Another diary entry is January 14, 1909. "He relishes that peasant wench with her strong body and her sunburnt legs; she allures

93

him just as powerfully now and she did all those years ago . . ."
Sonya wrote those words when Axinya was 80 years old. For half
a century, jealousy and an inability to forgive had blinded her, and
in the process destroyed her love for her husband.

Sonya's anguish is understandable. She was terribly hurt by the
man she loved. Her jealousy and bitterness and desire for revenge
are natural. People should get what they deserve. If they have hurt
others, they themselves should be hurt. W.H. Auden wrote about
this instinctual state of affairs in a little stanza:

I and the public know
What all school children learn,
Those to whom evil is done
Do evil in return.

In a piece I read in *The Globe and Mail*, the author was speaking
about a young Christian woman, of Arab descent. Her face was
pretty and fresh, almost cherubic, in fact. The author quoted her
as saying, "If I could, I would exterminate every Jew from the face
of the earth." It would, I'm sure, be possible to also find young
Jews who have lost friends and family in Palestinian attacks to say
the same things about those of Arab descent. When one is on the
receiving end of such violence and cruelty, hatred and the desire
for revenge seem the most natural of human responses. In fact, it
is the path humanity has chosen for millennia, personally and
collectively. It is why so little ever changes.

I was thinking about this, as I read the passage from the Acts of
the Apostles. Peter stands up to preach and he gives a summation
of the gospel of Jesus Christ. God sent a message of peace to the
people of Israel in Jesus Christ. The message spread, beginning with
John the Baptist's announcement that God had anointed Jesus with

the Holy Spirit and with power to do good and heal the sick. He was crucified, but God raised him up on the third day and allowed him to appear to certain witnesses, and to testify that he is the judge of the living and the dead. Everyone knows that all those who believe this receive forgiveness of sin, through his name.

It's the *Cole's Notes* of the gospel. But I was struck at how the whole gospel story leads up to that last sentence. Believers receive forgiveness of sin. It made me think, "Ah, so this is how God does it." This is how God manages to stay in loving relationship with the world.

We naturally focus on our own hurts and our own betrayals but we forget about the betrayal of God. Creation sullied, an uninterrupted reign of violence, injustice everywhere you turn, covenants repeatedly broken. There's a little saying, "love like you'll never get hurt," which is what God has been doing since the beginning of creation. But in the process, Love itself has been hurt. And if God were merely just, there would be a cosmic meltdown. Life itself would be like a bad *Rambo* movie, in which the offended one goes on a justified rampage of retaliation, until the score is settled, and then the whole thing would start all over with the next offence.

But that's not what happens. According to the gospel of Jesus Christ, God responds to repeated betrayal with forgiveness. The incarnation of God in Jesus Christ is itself God's initial act of forgiveness. We know how it ended, with Divine Love hanging from a cross. God taking the betrayals and atrocities of the centuries into Godself, and suffering them rather than repaying them. And that, we're asked to believe, is the divine strategy for the spiritual evolution of God's creation. That's the "new thing" that the prophet Isaiah is talking about. That's the way the former things pass away, so that a new reality can be birthed.

Hannah Arendt, a Jewish philosopher, covered the Nuremburg Trials when a man named Adolph Eichmann was on trial. She wrote a book about it, *Eichmann in Jerusalem.* She heard witness after witness describe what this man had done for the Nazis, most of which he refused to take responsibility for. Nevertheless, at the end, she came to the conclusion that the only remedy for the inevitability of history (and by this she meant the cycle of violence) was forgiveness. Otherwise, we remain trapped in what she called the "predicament of irreversibility." Without forgiveness, nothing new can happen, no future is possible which is not determined by the hurt and betrayals and violence of the past. Without forgiveness, eternity is nothing more than an endless repetition of the "former things."

In a novel by François Mauriac, *The Knot of Vipers,* a husband and wife spend the last decades of their life sleeping in separate rooms because a rift developed 30 years previously over whether the husband had shown enough care when their daughter fell ill. Neither husband nor wife was willing to forgive the other. Nothing new could happen, no new expression of love, no joint projects, no enjoyment of each other, or delight in life in that relationship as long as neither took the initiative to forgive.

When we say that we believe in Jesus Christ, one of the core things we're saying is that we believe in the divine strategy of forgiveness as the way to a new heaven and a new earth. And the scariest word in the whole Bible is two letters long. It's in the Lord's Prayer, right when we say "forgive us our sins . . . As we forgive others." Because being forgiven, being offered a new life is only the beginning for the Christian. We know ourselves to be forgiven sinners, and as such we're called to this most unnatural of enterprises, forgiving those who hurt and offend us. We become co-conspirators with God in transforming the former things into the new things God intends.

We were given a coffee table book for Christmas by my daughter, Sarah. It's called *Love*. It's a collection of the world's most powerful images having to do with love. One of the images is of Kim Phuc as a nine-year-old Vietnamese girl. It's perhaps the most widely recognized photo in the world, by photographer Nick Ut. She is naked, running away from a terrible fire with other children, a look of terror on her face. She recalls what happened just prior to this photo:

> One day everything changed. The war came to our village. My family hid for three days in the only "safe" haven, the nearby pagoda. When some soldiers saw the planes were going to bomb the holy place, they shouted to the children, "Get out. Run for it." I was so scared and I started running up the road with my cousins. Then I saw four bombs. Suddenly, there was napalm everywhere, and I was caught in the terrible fire. My clothes, my skin, burning. By some miracle, my feet weren't burned so I could run. I was screaming, "Nong qua! Nong qua!" Too hot, too hot.

That was June 1972, in the atrocity called the Vietnam War.

Because of her burns, Kim Phuc could not wear clothes on her upper body for over six months. Napalm is jellied gasoline. It burns deep under the skin, hotter than boiling water. For months when her nurses would have to peel off her layers of burned skin, she would pass out with pain. Altogether, she had to have 17 operations as a result of the Napalm. Kim is now living in Toronto, and, in 1997, she was appointed Goodwill Ambassador for UNESCO, giving her life to the pursuit of peace.

One day, she visited the Vietnam Veterans Memorial in Washington, DC. Here's what she says about it:

For what? Why did they have to suffer? Many veterans spoke with me. A man came out of the crowd and introduced himself. John Plummer told me he had been involved in planning the attack on my village, Trang Bang, the day I was burned. He said he had never forgiven himself and his life had been ruined. He asked me to forgive him, and I did. I think he was a victim, just like me. Another man, Mike, a helicopter door gunner in the war, told me he suffered terrible nightmares. As he talked, he wept. "All these years, I've held this photograph in my head . . . now I meet you and you forgive . . ."

When we receive the bread and wine in the sacrament of communion, we enter into a holy mystery. This sacrament has inexhaustible levels of meaning, but one of the simplest meanings is that, as we share it, we open to Christ's presence in a very deep way, in a way that can change us. At one level, in receiving Christ, we receive forgiveness. We are released from the former things, from whatever failures and betrayals and shame we've known. But in receiving the Christ, we're released for the new thing God is doing, which is the ongoing ministry of forgiveness, in and through us, the body of Christ.

An immigrant rabbi once told Philip Yancy that he had to forgive Adolph Hitler. He went on: "I did not want to bring Adolph Hitler inside me into my new country." There is a new country we're invited to inhabit. It is called the Kingdom of God. The road to it for us and all humanity is called forgiveness. Let us take this road together as we share the life of Jesus Christ in the sacrament of communion.

—January 20, 2002

Certain Women

LUKE 24:44-53; EPHESIANS 1:15-23

Arise then . . . women of this day!
Arise, all women who have hearts!
Whether your baptism be of water or of tears!
Say firmly:
"We will not have questions answered by irrelevant agencies,
  Our husbands will not come to us, reeking with carnage
For caresses and applause.
  Our sons shall not be taken from us to unlearn
All that we have been able to teach them of charity, mercy
    and patience.
  We, the women of one country,
Will be too tender to those of another country
To allow our sons to be trained to injure them . . ."

So begins the Mother's Day Proclamation, written in 1870 by Julia Ward Howe. She saw Mother's Day as a call to wives of warriors and mothers of sons to rise up against the violence of war. She was inspired by another woman of Appalachia, Anna Jarvis, who organized women throughout the Civil War to work for better sanitary conditions for both sides and went on to work for the reconciliation of Union and Confederate Neighbours. But it was Anna Jarvis's daughter who was successful in lobbying the state of West Virginia to establish Mother's Day. The tradition spread quickly throughout the US and, in 1914, President Woodrow Wilson declared the first national Mother's Day.

You'll look in vain these days in Hallmark card stores for one which calls mothers of the world to unite against war. Breakfast in bed, or brunch at Seasons in the Park is not exactly what the founders had in mind. Still, thank God we do stop to honour mothers this day.

I remember one night in Moose Jaw, Saskatchewan, as a young boy, throwing up most of the night, my mother at my side through the whole ordeal. That was the moment it dawned on me that she really must love me, to stay by my side and wipe my brow all through the messy night. Mother's Day is an opportunity to affirm and celebrate the power of the feminine spirit which manifests in mothering love across this planet and is alive in the fierce commitment to peace and justice. Julia Ward Howe, mother and activist, wrote one of the most famous hymns of all times: The Battle Hymn of the Republic. It was an anti-slavery hymn, intended to bolster the flagging spirits of the Union troops. She went on to be a leader in the fight for the vote for women.

Some say that the origins of Mother's Day go back even further. The ancient Greeks had a custom of Mother worship, a festival to Cybele, a great mother of gods. This custom is said to have spread throughout the Mediterranean basin. Religious intuition throughout the ages has always honoured the presence of this fierce feminine spirit at work in creation and in the world. Biblical scholar Elaine Pagels points out that a curious feature of the Jewish, Muslim and Christian God is the relative absence of the feminine divine. As portrayed in much of the Bible, ours is a jealous god, sharing no power with female deities, nor was he the divine lover of any. Contrast this with the religions of Egypt, Babylonia, Greece, Rome, Africa, India and indigenous people across the planet, all of which feature feminine deities.

The Gnostic gospels, carefully excluded from the collection of writings we call the New Testament, were more likely to portray God as both Father and Mother. Many of these writings gave priority to the feminine aspect of God, following the common sense observation that it is the feminine principle which gives birth to all of life.

However, in those churches committed to male authority structures, you won't find lively conversations going on about God as Mother. They know too well that once a feminine metaphor is used for God in heaven, power arrangements begin to shift here on earth. No longer is there any logical or theological rationale for men being the head of the household, or for not having a woman as Pope. If God is Mother as well as Father, what contrivance justifies the hoarding of power by men in red cloaks?

In Luke's gospel this morning, notice how women are mentioned as a kind of postscript. After carefully naming all eleven disciples, minus Judas Iscariot, Luke writes, "All these were devoting themselves to prayer, together with certain women, including Mary, the mother of Jesus . . ." These "certain women" don't rate a name, except for Mary, Jesus' mother. Indeed, Mary has had to carry most of the freight when it comes to honouring the feminine in the Christian tradition.

Father is still our default image of God, especially for those who've grown up in the church. It's "Our Father" in heaven, not our mother, and all attempts to change this have to pass through the neural network in our brain circuitry which throws up a father image for God on the screen of our minds. How did this happen? Elaine Pagels has traced the history of how the feminine divine was squeezed out of existence early in church history by the fathers of our faith.

It wasn't until the year 200, approximately, that our church fathers determined which books in the New Testament were in and which were out. It's news to some that there were many, many more gospels in circulation after the death of Jesus than the ones that comprise our Bible. One of those gospels is named after a "certain woman," the Gospel of Mary Magdalene. It features an argument between Mary and Peter. Dr. Pagels summarizes one of the encounters in the Gospel of Mary as follows:

> When the disciples, disheartened and terrified after the crucifixion, asked Mary to tell them what Jesus has told her secretly, she agrees, and teaches them, until Peter, furious, asks, "Did he really speak privately with a woman and not openly to us? Are we to turn about and all listen to her? Did he prefer her to us?" Distressed at his rage, Mary replies, "My brother Peter, what do you think? Do you think that I thought this up myself in my heart or that I am lying about the Saviour?" The other disciples intervene and convince a wounded Peter that Mary has authority to teach and that indeed the Lord loved her more. (The Gnostic Gospels, pp. 77-78)

Another argument appears in Pistis Sophia (Faith Wisdom), between Mary and Peter. Mary announces, "Peter makes me hesitate; I am afraid of him, because he hates the female race." Jesus replies that whomever the Spirit inspires is divinely ordained to speak, whether man or woman. (Pistis Sophia 36:71)

Orthodox Christians retaliated with letters and dialogues, inserted and falsely attributed to St. Paul, in 1 and 2 Timothy, Colossians, Ephesians, and Titus of our New Testament. These insertions and attributions contend that God forbids women to speak up in church or take positions of leadership. By the time our gospels were written, the power structures of the church had just about succeeded in relegating "certain women" to a "tag-along" status.

Almost, but not quite. The good news is that feminine imagery could not be expunged totally from the Bible. The feminine divine can be repressed but never eliminated. She makes an appearance as Sophia in Proverbs and Wisdom. Women are there at the cross, when others have fled; they are the first to the tomb after the crucifixion; women are the first to witness the resurrection. They show up in Luke's gospel as "certain women." It is clear that Jesus honoured women, challenging the patriarchal norms of his culture by including them among his disciples, conversing openly with them in public. When Mary anointed his feet with expensive oil, Jesus said that, because of this act, whenever the gospel is proclaimed she would be remembered. The fact that the writers of the gospel cannot leave them out of the story completely testifies to the historicity of Jesus' inclusion of women among his disciples and friends.

Two of the disciples in our reading from Acts stand gazing into the heavens as Jesus is being lifted up to sit at the right hand of God. Two men in white robes ask them why they are staring off into heaven. Jesus, they assure him, "will come in the same way you saw him go into heaven." Today is called Ascension Sunday. It was the gospel writers' way of getting Jesus off-stage after the resurrection. We should not be asking ourselves whether it's true that Jesus lifted off like some NASA launch. The question is: What did it mean to the early church?

Simply this: that all that Jesus stood for and proclaimed while on earth was now lifted up as eternally and universally authoritative, high above all pretenders to the throne, high above and more enduring than all principalities and powers, says Paul; high above and destined to prevail over the rulers and leaders of every age who cling to their own privilege and status at the expense of others; whites over blacks, rich over poor, straights over gays, men over women, human beings over the rest of creation. The Spirit of Christ, not Caesar, reigned and was the radical claim of the Ascension stories (Ephesians 1:15-23).

To say that the risen Christ was lifted up into the heavens and is sitting at the right hand of God is to celebrate, on this Mothering Sunday, that the feminine is lifted up with the Christ and in Christ. Christ's reign prevails in acts of justice, when compassion takes precedence over dominance, when the left-behinds are gathered up and given seats of honour, when women the world over are granted equal status, and when gentle mothers wipe the fevered brows of their children. To say that he will come again is to say that the fierce feminine spirit of the Christ, present in Jesus, is loose in every age and incarnates in souls offended by injustice and moved by mercy. Christ will come again and again to "trample out the vintage where the grapes of wrath are stored." The Christ will return until "certain women" are given names in sacred texts, and until the Mothering God who gave us birth is celebrated. We'll give Julia Ward Howe, mother of Mother's Day, the final word:

From the voice of a devastated Earth a voice goes up with
   our own.
It says, "Disarm! Disarm!
The sword of murder is not the balance of justice."
Blood does not wipe out our dishonour,
nor violence indicate possession.
As men have often forsaken the plough and the anvil
at the summons of war,

Let women now leave all that may be left of home

For a great and earnest day of counsel…

Whereby the great human family can live in peace,

each bearing after his own time the sacred impress, not of

   Caesar,

But of God.

—May 8, 2005

The Lord's Prayer:
A Blueprint for Peace

LUKE 11:1-13

A little boy prayed for a new pair of cowboy boots. One night he refused to say his prayers. His mother asked, "Why won't you say your prayers?"

"Art doesn't listen," he confided.

"Art who?" asked Mom.

"Art in heaven."

In Luke's Lord Prayer, there is no "art in heaven." Luke's Jesus doesn't give God a home address. Jesus addresses God as simply "Father." Luke presents us with the *Cole's Notes* of the Lord's Prayer. It's bare bones. This leads many scholars to think that it is the most original version of all the gospels.

But I'm getting a little ahead of myself. This morning I want to simply walk through this familiar prayer and try to mine it for its meaning. It's too easy to rattle it off Sunday after Sunday, without thinking about it much. There's a story about a little girl who prayed every night before she went to bed the familiar prayer, "Now I lay me down to sleep, I pray the Lord my soul to keep." One night, she too told her Daddy, "I'm not going to pray tonight." "Why not?" asked her father. "Well, every night I say the same prayer. When God comes to my house to listen, he must say, 'Here's where Laurel lives, and I already know exactly what she's going to say'."

So there are all kinds of reasons not to pray. Sometimes, we don't get what we want, like the little boy, and we turn away from

106

God in our hurt. Other times, like with the little girl, it just seems like we're not getting through anyway. The words seem to leave our lips and return to us empty. So what's the point? Or we're too busy, or have no privacy. All very real reasons. I've used them all myself. And sometimes it's simply that we don't know how to get started. This was the case with the disciples. They go to Jesus and say, "Lord, teach us how to pray." Now I don't believe for a moment that they had never prayed. As good Jews, they would have prayed in the synagogue since they were little children. It was a prerequisite in Jewish law, not an elective. So, I think when they asked him to teach them, they were really asking him to teach them to pray like that, like you do, not because you should but because you want to. Teach us to pray, in other words, as if God were real and heard our prayers.

Jesus starts the prayer by addressing God as "Father." There is much consternation these days among us, and I include myself, who feel free to call God "Mother" as well. Can we get over this, please? Jesus refers to himself elsewhere in the gospel as a mother hen, and no thinking person takes him literally. He's not saying he's really a mother hen, but rather that he has within him the qualities and characteristics of a hen with her chicks. In the same way, God is not literally a father or a mother, and Jesus certainly didn't think so. Rather, God relates to us the way a loving mother or father relates to children.

A devastating fire destroyed a large section of Yellowstone National Park in the late 1980s. A park ranger walked through the destroyed area afterwards and saw a bird literally petrified in the ashes, perched like a small statue at the base of a tree. Somewhat sickened by the sight he poked at it with his walking stick, and three baby birds scurried out from under the wings of their dead mother. The loving mother's instinct to protect her babies was more powerful than the instinct to fly away from the fire. This approaches what Jesus meant by addressing God as Divine Parent.

Jesus is getting at the nature of this God to whom we are addressing our prayers. This is no watchmaker God, who simply got the mechanisms of life going at the beginning of creation and then left it alone to tick away by itself for eternity. We pray to a God who cares about us personally and who loves us personally. I remember teaching a course on cosmology, and pointing out that there are at least one trillion galaxies in the Universe, each galaxy having on the order of 100 billion stars. A star is a million times larger than the earth. One woman almost had a nervous breakdown, because she immediately felt so insignificant. She felt smaller and more insignificant than a grain of sand on Long Beach, nothing more than an accident of life in this unimaginably enormous and uncaring Universe. If Jesus is right, however, the Universe is anything but indifferent. At the centre of the Universe beats a heart that loves us and wants to give us our deepest needs and wants. That's what Jesus means when he calls God "Father."

"Hallowed be thy name." There is a natural reverence that is evoked in the presence of this kind of love. This reverence is intended to be reserved for that which is truly holy. When this reverence is directed towards cars and lifestyles and money and athletes, it is called idolatry in Judaism. In Jesus' day, Caesar demanded that his name be hallowed as divine. Fundamentally, this line in the Lord's Prayer is subversive. It is intended that we place the emphasis on "thy." Hallowed be "thy" name and no other. As we pray this with understanding, we withdraw our idolatrous attachments to all that is not God, and in so doing we are returned to the path of holiness and right living.

"Thy Kingdom come." Again, we are meant to emphasize

"thy." Caesar's kingdom was already present. The whole world was living under its power and its rule. As Jesus formulated it, the Kingdom of God is what the world would look like, here and now, if it were under God's power and God's rule, in contrast to what it looks like under Caesar's power and rule.

Under Caesar, peace is maintained through the use or the threat of violence. Under God's rule, violence is not an option. Under Caesar, some get very rich while the vast majority remains very poor. This arrangement was believed to be divinely ordained. Under God's rule, this arrangement is a travesty of justice and compassion, and will be overturned. Under Caesar's rule, the privileged are served. Under God's rule, the privileged are servants.

Under Caesar's rule, there is room at the table only for those of the right gender (namely male), the right class, and the right social status and sexual orientation. Under God's rule, the table is wide open; there is a radical egalitarianism that breaks down all these distinctions. Caesar still rules today in the 21st century. Praying for God's Kingdom to come is as relevant today as it was in Jesus' day. You understand that Caesar is not at all supportive of this particular petition, which is why Jesus said that those who followed him would have to be willing to carry their cross.

"Give us this day our daily bread." After prayers for the big picture, Jesus gets more personal. We are encouraged to pray for our own needs to be met for this very day. We shouldn't label it as selfishness to ask God for what we need. In the asking there is an acknowledgement of our dependence. Jesus asks for bread, and we can take this both literally and symbolically. As an itinerant, Jesus was dependent on others for food. On a symbolic level, asking God for bread is about being conscious of what we need this very day to sustain us. Is it patience with our colleague at work? Is it strength to suffer an illness with grace? Is it to be shown that you are loveable and worthwhile by one person? Is it the power to get through one more day without alcohol? It is not only okay to ask God for what we need; it breaks down the illusion of self-sufficiency and cultivates an attitude of gratitude for God's gifts.

"Forgive us our sins for we ourselves forgive everyone who is indebted to us." In her book *Speaking of Sin*, Barbara Brown Taylor writes:

> To measure the full distance between where we are and where God created us to be—suffer that distance, to name it, to decide not to live quietly with it any longer—that is the moment when we know we are dead and begin to decide who we will be tomorrow. When I say "sin" there is no telling what you see: the stolen candy bar, the rumpled sheets of a bed you shared with someone else's mate, a large pipe spilling orange sludge into a once-blue river, a clutch of homeless people sitting around a fire built in a vacant lot between sky-scrapers. The picture will be different for every one of you, but the experience to hunt for is the one that makes part of you die.

Sin is broken relationship, with self, other, the earth and God. The only way to restore these broken relationships is through forgiveness. Forgiveness is the willingness to put restorative justice ahead of retributive justice. It alone breaks the violent cycle of an eye for an eye, and a tooth for a tooth. God's primary concern is with mending relationships, not meting out punishment or collecting on debts owed. Jesus was in the world reconciling the world with God, not to punish the world for sinning against God. That's why the last thing he did before he was executed was to forgive his executors. Because the heart of God beat within him, he couldn't bear the pain of their being so desperately alienated from God. That's why we forgive in Christ's name, because the pain of being out of relationship with those who have hurt us exceeds the pain they have caused us.

"And do not bring us into the time of trial." This is a better translation than "lead us not into temptation," which always makes me ask the question, "Why would God do that anyway?" A more accurate translation of the original Aramaic, according to Aramaic scholar Neil Douglas-Klodtz, would be "don't let us enter" or "don't let us be seduced by appearances." There is no suggestion of any outside power who leads us into temptation or brings us to the time of trial. Jesus is talking about an inner experience of vacillation, of encountering the seductions of a world and a culture which we allow to tempt us away from our core purpose and meaning in life.

"Deliver us from evil." In Aramaic, the word *bisha* means evil or error in the sense of inappropriate action. Wrong action manifests when we vacillate and stray from divine purpose. Jesus is teaching us to pray to be delivered from whatever holds us back from discovering and embracing our divine purpose, from walking the divine path.

"For yours is the kingdom, and the power and the glory for ever and ever." I have already commented on Jesus' subversive ministry of non-violently divesting Caesar of his claims to kingdom, power, and glory, and shifting these claims to the sovereign God, where they belong. "For ever and ever," is far too abstract a translation. In the Aramaic it implies "until our next gathering." Jesus knew that this subversive activity of centering our lives in God is difficult. We need to re-gather the community of faith on a weekly basis, to re-member who we are and whose we are.

"Amen." This word sealed agreements in the Middle East. It was a solemn oath and conferred power on whatever preceded it.

The Lord's Prayer is a prescription for peace in our lives and in our world. To live with the awareness that we are deeply loved by God (which is to know God as divine mother and father) is the foundation of peace. To envision what the world would be like, what our lives would be like, if God ruled (which is to pray for the Kingdom of God) is the work of peace. To revere what is truly sacred (which is to hallow God's name) is the work of peace. To transform violence into suffering, rather than suffering into violence (which is the challenge of forgiveness), is the work of peace. To center our lives in our divine purpose and stay the course when the seductions of the world tempt us away is the work of peace. With the disciples we approach our Lord and ask, "Jesus, teach us to pray like this."

—July 29, 2001

On Being Rich Toward God

LUKE 12:13-21

"For one's life does not consist in the abundance of possessions."

I find myself listening more and more to these phone-in radio programs. You know the ones—call Dr. Laura or Dr. Joy—and as long as you're willing to lay your private life out for a couple of million listeners and be humiliated by the doctor who lets you know how utterly stupid you were in the first place for getting into this problem, as long as you're willing to do this, they are more than happy to give you the precise piece of advice that's going to change your life instantly. What fascinates me is the good doctor's apparent confidence in reducing a complex life situation to a single, simple intervention. The other side of my fascination is with the willingness of the callers to comply, at least on air, and then express their undying appreciation for this abuse.

So it is with great interest that I read from Luke's gospel today. Some fellow in a crowd has a problem. His brother won't share the inheritance with him, and he wants Jesus to solve his problem. We've all seen what these inheritances can do to families, haven't we? It's a real problem. So he wants Dr. Jesus to tell his brother to do the right thing, and share it with him.

Unlike our modern-day on-air therapists, Jesus is having no part of it. "Man, who made me judge or arbitrator over you?" And this gets to the nub of the disservice some of these modern-day advice dispensers offer to their callers. Jesus is not going to rob this man of the opportunity that his life situation presents him with to do some deep reflection. It's a soul issue, you see. Reflection is a lost art in our time-impoverished culture. The soul loves to sink its teeth into the marrow of a problem until a blessing is wrested in the form of wisdom. This man should be consulting his soul about this issue. His soul would have all kinds of questions to help him reflect on this crisis. "How will your envy and your anger affect the rest of your life?" "What does the inheritance bring up for you around your relationship with your father?" "What exactly do you need the inheritance for?" "What does money mean to you?" Et cetera. You get the idea. If Jesus were to simply say, "Listen, friend, put your brother on the line and I'll sort him out. I'll tell that good-for-nothing what a good man should do for his little brother," this man would have lost the opportunity for soul work.

So Jesus doesn't offer advice, but he does issue a warning that gives the man a strong hint about the subject area for reflection. "Be very, very careful." You see, Jesus knows that what's at stake here is this man's soul. "Be on guard against all kinds of greed." All "kinds" of greed? You mean greed isn't just about money? Greed issues from a perception of scarcity. If I believe that there is not going to be enough to go around, then my ego begins to gather things up and store them away like a squirrel getting ready for winter. It's possible to be greedy about anything for which we believe there's a shortage. It could be love. I'll grab onto it and by God won't let anyone get away with not loving me. I'll do whatever I have to do, get sick, get rich, get smart, in order to have it.

Jesus warned against "all kinds of greed." Ronald Rolheisser, a Catholic theologian, speaks about the modern spiritual disease of restlessness. Driven by a perception of scarcity, we experience a chronic discontent with what is within our grasp, with what we have here and now, so we reach out for more and more. He talks about a greed for experience. "Our lives become consumed with the idea that unless we somehow experience everything, travel everywhere, see everything, know everyone, then our own lives are small and meaningless."

Think of our children these days. Think how we cater to their greed for experience; like their boomer parents they want it all, and now. They can't wait. They travel around the world at a very young age, have every kind of consumer object; they are exposed to whatever movies and videos or video games they desire, dating at age 12, sex at age 15 . . . and then as Rolheisser says, "we wonder why they are bored, cynical, and fatigued in spirit at age 20."

I remember one of my pastoral counseling supervisors writing an evaluation about me. It said something like, "Bruce has a lot of talent, no question, but I am concerned that he will have done everything in the field and read everything by the time he is 35, and become bored." I didn't have a clue what he was talking about. He was talking about a kind of greed related to time, which I still have. Something inside tells me that I have to do it all now or else there won't be enough time to fit it all into one lifetime. I want to fit six lifetimes into one life. Do you hear the perception of scarcity as it relates to time? So my generation has learned to "multitask"—to talk on the phone while cooking dinner, with the golf on TV, and at the same time write a message to Ann to peel the carrots. The irony is that, in my greediness to create more time, I miss the present moment. I've missed God's glimpse of eternity in the here and now.

But of course greed is also about money. Who among us has not wanted more of the stuff? I must admit I love those 6/49 lottery billboards. "Honey, the bank manager is not being very nice to us," but the "not" has been crossed out, leaving, "the bank manager is being very nice to us." What has changed of course is that in the interim, they've won the lottery. We have this fundamentalist solution as a cure to all our problems. More money. We'll be happy and secure when we have that $2 million tucked away for our retirement. But there's never enough of it. At last count Bill Gates had personal wealth equivalent to that of 43% of the total American population.

The rich farmer in Jesus' parable has a problem: too much grain, nowhere to stash it. Notice what he does with his problem. "He thought to himself . . . 'What should I do with my crops?' Then he said, 'I know, I'll make bigger barns so I have room for even more grain, and then I will say to my soul, Soul, you have ample goods laid up for many years; relax, eat, drink, and be merry'."

Please, let's not confuse this inner dialogue with what I referred to earlier as reflection. He makes a decision, and then tells his soul what he's going to do. Make no mistake, friends. He has not consulted his soul on this one. It was pure unadulterated ego chatter. If he had consulted his soul, that deeply human part of us which is connected to God, self, and neighbour, who knows what he might have heard? His soul might have told him to ask the beggar he passes en route to market every weekend what he should do with his excess. His soul might have suggested that he go pay a visit to his childhood friend, who hasn't been so fortunate. You see, this man's got a hole in his soul as big as that barn he's going to build, and no amount of grain or wealth is going to fill it up. That hole is meant to be filled by God alone, and if he had a soul he could do a consultation. But he's lost it. That's what greed does to us. As soon as it takes over, whether it's greed for love, or more time or money, we lose our connection to God, to our soul, to other human beings, and to the earth.

The problem, of course, is not with wealth per se. Some people are born into it, some inherit it, and some just know how to make it. Nothing is wrong with that. But we are naïve if we imagine that just because some people have more of it than we do, or because we have more of it in the Western world than two-thirds of the world's population, that our problems are solved. We are in danger of losing our souls. No, the problem is not with getting wealth; it's giving it back freely and joyfully. Money only brings us life and joy when it's circulating freely through us. The farmer received a free gift of wealth in the form of good crops. But he consciously cut off the circulation process and built bigger barns. That pretty much describes what the Western world has done with our good fortune. The earth gives freely; we take and take and take, to the point of degradation, but return only these paltry sums of money for restoration. Governments continually reduce the amount of foreign aid in our budgets, and when we do give it, it's often with all kinds of strings attached. Our relative wealth leaves us with a problem—a problem that Jesus leaves us with to sort out.

"You fools," says Jesus, "this very night your life is being demanded of you. And the things you have prepared, whose will they be? So it is with those who store up treasures for themselves but are not rich toward God." David Buttrick tells a modern-day equivalent of Jesus' parable. There was a man who thought he had the future licked. By some magic he had gotten hold of a copy of *The New York Times* dated a year in advance. What a bonanza! He knew what stocks to buy and sell, what properties to purchase. He rubbed his hands together with glee, until he turned a page and read his own obituary.

The American Benefactor is a magazine that calculated which Americans had donated the most money to interests and causes. Many names were familiar, but there was one whom nobody recognized—Charles F. Feeney, 66. He made his money from duty-free shops, like the ones we see at international airports. He gives to schools, colleges, hospitals, and youth programs in the US and Ireland. Maureen Dowd wrote about him in *The New York Times*. Feeney gives anonymously, she reports. His family happily watches him give away most of their inheritance. He gives not aristocratically but in the conviction that we should keep only what we need. He owns no house or car; he flies economy and wears a $15 watch, which keeps perfect time, he told her. Ms. Dowd reports: "He was thrilled to be dropped from *Forbes* list of the richest Americans this year because he has given so much money away" (*Christian Century*, December 24-31, 1997).

St. Paul says, "If you have been raised with Christ, seek the things that are above; set your mind on those things, not on things of earth." I don't know if Mr. Feeney is a religious man or not, but I do know that he has discovered the secret of being "rich toward God." Let us open our hearts, our hands, and our minds, trusting that God freely gives all that we need for life.

—*August 5, 2001*

You Have Heard It Said

MATTHEW 5:38-48

*"You have heard it said that you shall love your neighbour and
hate your enemy. But I say to you. Love your enemies and pray
for those who persecute you."*

We continue to struggle to comprehend the magnitude of
the tragedy of September 11. Memorial services replace
vigils of hope, as many nations and many families come to terms
with a terrible reality. Emily Dickinson's words ring true once
again, "The morning after death / Is solemnest of industries / Enacted upon earth." Thousands and thousands of people are being
laid off in the airline industry, and those who support this industry. I could never have imagined that for my close friend, Bruce
Bennet, a captain for Air Canada, his workplace could become a
potential weapon of mass destruction. The last time Dow Jones
lost as much in a week was in the Great Depression. The spectre
of chemical warfare is raised in newspaper articles and magazines.
Only two weeks ago, we knew what it was to feel relatively safe.
And in one act of unimaginable terror, our world seems to be
spinning out of control.

As I was preparing this sermon, William Butler Yeats's poem
The Second Coming came to mind:

Turning and turning in the widening gyre
the falcon cannot hear the falconer;

Things fall apart; the centre cannot hold;
Mere anarchy is loosed upon the world,
The blood-dimmed tide is loosed, and everywhere
the ceremony of innocence is drowned;
The best lack all conviction, while the worst
Are full of passionate intensity.

Indeed. The "passionate intensity" of terrorist hatred has loosed a "blood-dimmed tide." And into this anarchy, into our anger and our need to make someone, somewhere pay for this, we hear the words of Jesus:

You have heard it said, 'an eye for an eye, and a tooth for a tooth'. But I say to you, 'Do not resist an evildoer'. . . if any-one strikes you on the right cheek, turn the other cheek also; You have heard it said, 'You shall love your neighbour and hate your enemy.' But I say to you, 'Love your enemies and pray for those who persecute you, so that you may be chil-dren of your Father in heaven . . . for he makes the sun rise on the evil and on the good, and sends the rain on the righ-teous and the unrighteous. For if you love those who love you, what reward do you have . . . be perfect, therefore, even as your heavenly Father is perfect . . .'

These are words we do not want to hear at a time like this. They simply ask too much of us. This is a perfection that eludes most of us. Couldn't we just ignore these few verses, and get on with what comes naturally to us? We cannot believe that anyone, even Jesus, would turn the other cheek in response to what has happened in New York and Washington. Love these terrorists? We loathe them.

The problem is that it is a spiritual principle that if we respond out of hatred we will breed more hatred. When we respond out of hatred we are no longer "children of our Father in heaven." In first-century cosmology there were only two options. Either one was a child of Satan, who is the father of murder and lies, or one was a child of God, in whom is only love. Love for even those who are our enemies. And this is what is almost impossible, from a purely natural point of view, to fathom. "God makes the sun rise on the evil and on the good, and sends rain on the righteous and on the unrighteous." God loves Osama bin Laden is what we're being asked to believe here. God detests what he has done, if indeed he is behind the tragedy, but still loves him. Let me reiterate, this seems as unnatural to me as I'm sure it does to you. But our first response to the kind of hatred we have experienced is to be stewards of our own souls. If all we can muster is hate, then the terrorists have won the spiritual battle before we've even begun.

I came across a paragraph written by Martin Luther King Jr., which stopped me in my tracks:

> To our most bitter opponents we say: we shall match your capacity to inflict suffering by our capacity to endure suffering. We shall meet your physical force with soul force. Do to us what you will, and we shall continue to love you. We cannot in all good conscience obey your unjust laws, because non-cooperation with evil is as much a moral obligation as is cooperation with good. Throw us in jail and we shall still love you. Bomb our homes and threaten our children, and we shall still love you. Send the Ku Klux Klan into our communities at the midnight hour and beat us and leave us half dead, and we shall still love you. But be ye assured that we will wear you down by our capacity to suffer. One day we shall win freedom, but not

only for ourselves. We shall so appeal to your heart and conscience that we shall win you in the process, and our victory
will be a double victory.

I hear that and I don't know whether to laugh or cry. I feel so far
from the spiritual depth of the man who wrote those words that I
wonder if I can even call myself a Christian. "Be perfect,
therefore, as your heavenly Father is perfect," Jesus admonishes
us. But I'm not perfect. I feel like St. Paul, who was driven almost
crazy by the high ethical demands of Jewish Law. He couldn't live
up to them. They convicted him day in, day out, as a sinner.
Eventually, of course, it was the impossibility of him ever being
able to attain these high standards that brought him to God. He
thought he could achieve perfection under his own steam, by his
own willpower. He couldn't. He needed Christ. Jesus has set the
bar too high for us as well.

This ethic of love has the power to bring us back to a radical dependence on God's grace for the capacity to hold onto our love,
when everything in us feels justified in hating.

Make no mistake. We will end up hating if we do not throw ourselves upon the Source of all love, and if we end up hating, we cannot serve the cause of peace. A man leaving a memorial service for
the victims of the September 11 tragedy tells a CNN reporter, "I'm
supposed to be Christian, but my prayers are for revenge." Graf-
fiti near a mosque in England reads, "Avenge the USA, kill a Muslim." Attacks on mosques have been widely reported across
Europe, the US and Canada. A brown-skinned acquaintance intervenes in a ruckus caused by three young teenagers, and one of
them reacts, "Who do you think you are anyway, you Paki!" In
London, a taxi driver is left a quadriplegic after being dragged
from his cab and beaten by three men. President Bush deserves

credit for clearly signaling that the enemy is terrorism, not the Muslim faith. But still, let's face it; without going to a deeper spiritual well, this world will spin out in a blood-dimmed tide of hatred.

For Jesus, turning the other cheek didn't mean passive acquiescence to terror. It meant finding creative responses to violence, which at one and the same time undermined the power of the perpetrator and left the dignity and the spirituality of the victim intact. Being struck on the right cheek, for example, was only possible with a backhand blow. First-century Mediterranean culture was a right-handed culture. Hitting with the back of the right hand was used by the dominant class to humiliate the underclass. To offer the other cheek would require the perpetrator to use an open hand or a fist, which is how one fought with a person of equal social status. The receiver of the blow has thus robbed the oppressor of the power to humiliate.

To do nothing in response to the terrorists' actions would be playing into their hands. It would show them that the Americans are paralysed by fear. But the invitation of Jesus is to find creative responses to this violence that will accomplish two things: first, bring the perpetrators to justice and second, not bring us down to the same level of spiritual depravity as those who carried out this terror. Killing innocent bystanders in the pursuit of justice can find no more moral justification than the terrorists' killing of innocent people in New York and Washington.

A creative response might be to encourage the American government to take seriously the question of the gentleman from Pennsylvania after the third plane crashed: "Why do they hate us so much?" Much of this hate is irrational and based in an extremist fundamentalist ideology, no doubt. But not all of it. There is a moderate Muslim voice which can shed light on this question, and it needs to be listened to: this non-violent Muslim voice is telling the Western world that the injustices in Palestine are a source of intense rage in the Islamic world. As well, the presence of the US Army on Saudi soil is considered an insult to the Islamic faith. Now, please understand me here. I am in no way justifying the actions of the terrorists in New York. I am merely pointing out that the age-old response of going in and retaliating goes against the more complex demands of the gospel.

It is easy to forget that, as a Jewish peasant living under Roman occupation, Jesus had plenty of reason to hate. He was dirt poor, living at a subsistence level. His life was much closer to that of an Afghanistan peasant than to our own. On a whim, Roman soldiers could demand that a Jew stop what he was doing, anytime, anywhere, and carry their bags. The peasant and agrarian classes had been forced into unsupportable debt, and repossession of land by the wealthy because of inability to pay was commonplace. There were at least four Jewish terrorist movements that Jesus knew about. Most thought, in fact, that the Messiah would be a warrior, dedicated to the violent overthrow of the Romans. Jesus watched, along with his Jewish friends, hundreds of other Jews being executed by the Romans, by the most grotesque means known to humanity at the time, crucifixion. And of course, this was his fate. He had plenty of reason to choose hatred and retaliation as a response to violence, but in the end asphyxiating on the cross, he uttered his final words, "Father, forgive them, they know not what they are doing."

Imagine how tempting it was, after Jesus was executed by the Romans, for the disciples to join up with one of the terrorist organizations. It would have been easy to justify going underground and making their central mission the eradication of the Romans. But that's not what happened. It is nothing short of a miracle that their response was to carry on the mission of their teacher. The first thing they did was to pool their wealth and redistribute it according to need. You can read about it in the Acts of the Apostles. The second thing they did was to feed and house the poorest of the poor. When they themselves were rounded up, imprisoned, persecuted, and even executed, they responded to this with love. You will not find a single instance of retaliation in the entire New Testament, even though there was plenty of justification. Yes, it's a miracle. And no, it's not natural. It's supernatural. Their power to love came from beyond themselves.

What they experienced was that, when they came together to break bread, to share a common meal, to sing hymns and offer prayers, Christ was right there in their midst. And then they came to the astounding realization that they were Christ's body in the world, the visible incarnation of the very spirit of Christ. And this gave them power to love, when the natural thing to do was to hate. Let us gather at this table, friends, share a meal, and pray to be transformed in the image of our teacher, who died to show us another way.

—September 23, 2001

Dear God

GENESIS 4:8-16, 23-24, 6:11-13; MATTHEW 18:21-22

Now the earth was corrupt in God's sight, and the earth was filled with violence.

Dear God,
I'm writing to you because I don't understand what's going on in the world. I guess you've heard by now that we're starting the 21st century pretty much the way we spent most of the 20th century: killing each other. I'm a spiritual leader, you see, and people are expecting some answers from me. They come to church looking for an answer to why the world is so violent and what we're supposed to do about it. But the "honest-to-You" truth is that I'm filled with questions. I hope this is okay with you. I thought if I talked it over with you it might help.

First question: How does it happen that both Osama bin Laden and President Bush call each other evil? They both seem absolutely convinced that You are on their side. Both of them believe they're on the side of good and the side of truth. I guess that's what makes it possible for them to kill so many people.

I know what Osama bin Laden and the network of terrorists did is absolutely wrong. Several thousand people were murdered and he seems pretty happy about it. What happened to him, God? Was he born that way? I know I shouldn't care about a murderer, but it does matter to me. You see, I have to believe that we're all born in your image. If I believed some of us were born more evil than good, then it's really easy for me to support those who want to kill the evil ones. Truth be known, some of the stuff bin Laden says about the Palestinians and American foreign policy makes sense to me. I think it must have made sense to President Bush, too, because all of a sudden he's talking about giving the Palestinian people more support. But the thing is, God, Osama bin Laden doesn't represent those people who have been hurt by the Western world. He did this for his own reasons, and we may never know what they were, and apparently he has some biological weapons that he's not afraid to use. He's very lost, God, and very dangerous, and I don't want my daughter to die of bubonic plague. I'm afraid there's not much we can do to get through to him, so I'm asking you to try again.

The other thing, God, is that I've been doing all this reading about how the American government has done some terrible things in the past, too. I know someone who used to live in a country in Central America, and one morning she returned to her village and found all of her friends dead, killed by soldiers the CIA trained to overthrow a democratically elected government that was dedicated to land reform, which wasn't in America's national interests, whatever that means.

There's another bad man whose name is Saddam Hussein. He tried to invade Kuwait because he thought they were taking more than their fair share of oil. So then the US went to war against him because they had to make sure he didn't take more than his share of oil from them. We like oil a lot down here, God, enough to kill for it. So they've been bombing his country for ten years now and stopping supplies from getting through, and over a million people in Iraq have died. I watched a documentary in which Iraqi Christians were crying and asking what kind of Christianity we practiced in the West. I guess Saddam Hussein was asking for it, but if he's so bad then why did the Americans sell him billions of dollars of weapons in the 1980s? I guess it is one of those national interest issues again.

One more thing: Ten years ago, Osama bin Laden, he's the evil one I was talking about before, was best friends with the US government because he was helping them to fight the Russians. The CIA trained him, apparently, and they did a pretty good job. God, this is happening all the time on earth. If a government doesn't like what's happening in another part of the world, because it doesn't fit with their plan for the world, then they pay warlords and opposition militia to overthrow that government. Then they install the government they want. Is this okay, God? Because down here, we seem to just accept it. I've never been on the receiving end of that kind of treatment myself, but it would make me pretty angry if I had been.

We don't find out about this stuff very easily, but because of the Internet, you can read all about it. If you want, you can check it out on Znet. And I shouldn't really be talking about this much, in public, because if I do it's called "a left-wing rant," and what happens is that anyone who wants to talk about these things is told to go live in a cave with bin Laden if we love him and his way of life so much. We don't want to live there, God, and we abhor what bin Laden has done, but we do want to know what's true. The other thing is that we're accused of being anti-American, but God I've got nothing against the American people at all; it's the government that does these things that seem to be against the very principles they stand for.

The other big question I have God is whether you even want me to talk about this stuff. I mean it's not really "spiritual" is it? Sometimes I think people wish they could just come to church and all send positive thoughts into the atmosphere, and then go and be kind to each other, and just leave all these other political matters to people who know more about it than I do. But in the Bible, I notice that your prophets are always speaking truth to power, and power doesn't like it much. It's why Jesus got executed by the state. So I guess it's not so easy to separate the two.

I'm not saying I know the truth God; and in fact I'm afraid of people who think they do. It's just that I hate being lied to, and I feel so powerless. Please let me know if you want me to pursue this.

Honestly, God, I'm tempted to just give up, turn my back on the whole affair, find some good people and go live on an island, buy some massage tables, and start this whole bloody thing over. Do it right this time. That's what you did, eh God? I mean, start all over. I read it in Genesis. How the first death in the Bible was a cold-blooded murder. I've got a few questions about that, God. It says that you marked Cain so that if anyone was tempted to avenge Abel's death, you would kill seven others in retaliation. I know you did this to prevent the violence from escalating out of control. That was the idea anyway. But then only four generations later, Noah's dad, Lamech, kills a young man. And by this time, he threatens that if anyone tries to get him back, it will cost, not seven lives but seven times seventy lives. That strategy of retaliation didn't seem to be working so well.

That's what we're going through, down here, God. Iraq threatens our oil supplies, and we take a million of their lives. On MSN, they're even calling the news coverage of the war *America Strikes Back*. I guess the 3,000 people killed in New York are going to cost at least 210,000 lives. That's 3,000 times 70. That's just on their side. 'Cause they are using the same Bible as we are pretty much on this one, and so for everyone of those 210,000 lives we take, it's going to cost—well, I don't have a calculator God, and it's making me kind of sick and very sad to think about it much.

But when I read that part where it says that you looked down upon human beings and saw only evil and terrible violence and decided to start all over again, I could totally relate. Now, I know that's not how it really happened. I know that there probably was a Great Flood that killed lots of people, and when they tried to make sense of it, all they could figure was that it happened because you were mad at them. But it's interesting that the first thing that came to their minds about what made you so mad was all the violence.

One other question: Remember when Jesus was asked how many times we should forgive someone who hurts us. "As many as seven times?" one of his disciples asked. And Jesus answered, "seventy times seven." Remember that part? Well, was he thinking about cancelling out Lamech's strategy of retaliation there? Is this the mathematics of your Kingdom? Is that our choice—forgiveness or retaliation? I know this much, God. Retaliation hasn't worked. Even if we manage to kill Osama bin Laden, he'll become a martyr, just like Jesus, only what will rise up out of his ashes is more violence instead of more love. But forgiveness? How do we forgive what is unforgivable? How do we not hate them? Forgiveness is not going to make the terrorists go away. We're stuck, God, really stuck.

So, I want to run an idea past you. Maybe forgiveness means deciding to just start over, like you did. Not once and for all, but a renewed commitment the moment our feet hit the floor every new day. I'll never be able to figure out all the causes of what has happened, God. There are so many lies being told by both sides, that I'm getting really exhausted trying. I can tell you that. But I'm thinking if I just put all that energy instead into allowing you to create a new reality through me, and through this congregation, then we wouldn't feel so hopeless and helpless. And maybe that's what forgiveness means. Just feeling this great sorrow in my chest for how bloody lost we all are, and not letting what's happened in the past determine our future. Just letting it go.

Can I just give up trying figure out who the bad guys are and who the good guys are, and just know that evil has spread like a computer virus over the Internet, and it's infected our hearts because we were all selfish and stubborn, and greedy and pig-headed, and complacent? And what we need is a brand-new operating system because the old one is ruined. That's my idea, God; let me know what you think.

I have to go now, God. But here's my prayer: Send another flood. Only this time, make it a flood of tears. Forty days and forty nights of tears. A rain of tears. Your tears flowing through me and through all of us for what is happening again. Enough tears to cleanse our hearts; enough tears to lift us up and carry us into a new age; enough to give us the resolve to follow Jesus this time in the way of peace; to feed the hungry, heal the sick, comfort those who mourn, to forgive, to seek justice, to love kindness, and to walk humbly with you, and lightly upon this earth. God, I wish it would rain.

Your servant,
Bruce.

—*October 14, 2001*

Ahab's Sin, and Ours?

I KINGS 21

"Get up, eat some food and be cheerful;
I will give you the vineyard of Naboth."

This past week we celebrated the 73rd anniversary of the United Church of Canada, as I alluded to with the children. On Tuesday night at Spirit Song, I invited participants to share what they celebrated about our church. There was much to celebrate: our openness to diversity, our theological flexibility, our courage around issues of social justice, our concern for the larger world, not just our own, the wonderful sense of belonging in community.

I am sure that we could each add our own kudos. This year, however, the celebration is somewhat obscured by what we are hearing about the United Church of Canada and its role in the Residential School Systems, particularly in Port Alberni. I want to briefly address this issue this morning in light of the Scripture reading from the first book of Kings. A brief background to the case is in order, and I quote from an article in *Touchstone* magazine, written by Keith Howard and Gaye Sharpe:

> In this case, the United Church of Canada is facing a law suit brought by 30 First Nations people against the Government of Canada, the Church, and Mr. John Andrews, a former

principal at the Alberni Indian Residential School. Henry Arthur Plint, a dorm supervisor in the school in the late forties to the early sixties, was sentenced, in March 1995, to 11 years in prison for 18 sexual abuse-related convictions. The current legal proceedings are to determine the extent of "vicarious liability" which the Church and the federal government bear for the actions of Mr. Plint. You have by now heard that the ruling is that the United Church is jointly responsible with the federal government.

The way the issue has been reported this past week on the radio, it sounded as if the United Church of Canada, my church, was fighting tooth and nail to avoid financial responsibility for the victims of sexual and physical abuse. It was shocking to me to hear that we, who have been consistent and faithful outspoken advocates for victims, seemed to be trying to shirk responsibility and accountability. According to the article, written by two witnesses to the court proceedings, in the opening statement the United Church lawyer said that the church would accept no liability. We did attempt to settle, out of court, but only with the federal government, not the victims themselves. To make matters worse, the testimony of one First Nations man was challenged early in the proceedings by raising the spectre of "false memory." Keith Howard and Gaye Sharpe report feeling profound shame in the hallways of the courthouse between sessions, as witnesses expressed that, although they might expect a shirking of responsibility by the government, surely the church should operate from a higher moral code.

And then I read the story about King Ahab and Naboth. Ahab wanted Naboth's vineyard because it was near the royal estate and would make a great vegetable garden for him. The king would compensate him with money. But Naboth refused. Naboth's refusal was based on the fact that the land the king wanted was his ancestral inheritance. This gave him moral, religious, and political claim. This ancient story began to take on remarkable relevance as it relates to indigenous peoples, land claims, and the legacy of residential schools.

King Ahab is a fairly apt personification of the white man from the point of view of indigenous peoples, symbolized in this story by Naboth. Ahab, who holds all the cards, does not know what he is asking for. To him, Naboth's vineyard will make a nice vegetable garden to service him and his royal court. But to Naboth, the land is sacred. It is an ancestral inheritance and therefore part of his very identity. From the moment the Europeans set foot on the so-called "New World," they similarly showed very little awareness of the sacredness of the land for the indigenous peoples. They saw it as a source of gold and other precious minerals, spices, sugar, and timber. There was no sense that what was being taken was an ancestral inheritance that defined the indigenous people's very identity.

Naboth was "offed," which is what happens historically when those without power say "no" to the powerful. After Naboth's "no," King Ahab went to his room to sulk, and Queen Jezebel took over. She did the dirty work.

This offing of Naboth has both literal and symbolic parallels as it relates to our indigenous peoples. Massive numbers of native peoples were offed in a literal sense, killed in their struggle with white men over their land, or through contagious disease. But the death of Naboth is a symbol for another kind of offing, in which native persons were victims of another kind of cultural death.

The strategy of native assimilation popular in the 20th century has been ultimately harmful for native culture, language, and their very identity. The residential schools were a key component of this strategy. We need to remember that residential schools were conceived of as a compassionate solution to native poverty and illiteracy. The United Church cooperated with this strategy as the most creative solution to a very complex problem. Still, it is clear that, although some native persons speak out about how they were helped by residential schooling, overall it was a mistake. I ask you to imagine for a moment what it would be like to have your children taken from you and placed in these schools.

> Imagine that the shoe was on the other foot. Imagine a hundred years during which government policy removes our children from our homes when they reach elementary school age. Reports of hunger and disease surfaced in every decade of their existence. Then we find out that our children are forbidden to speak English, but must speak only the dominant aboriginal tongue. They are disciplined with a cane when they attempt to speak English. Siblings are separated, cannot talk together, or comfort each other. Celebration of Christian festivals is not tolerated; no Sunday worship, no Bible reading. Instead our children are forced to observe the aboriginal festivals. They are allowed to return home to see you only once a year, only to leave in tears as they return to school. After this entire attempt at assimilation, the children discover enormous racism, as whites are considered second-class citizens. And then we discover decades later the awful secret that many of our children have been the victims of sexual predators. Imagine. Is it any wonder the memory of the residential school system does not go away? (*Touchstone*, May 1998)

There are still other components of the Biblical story that are recognizable today. Take Ahab's unconsciousness. When Jezebel visits the sulking king in his room to deliver the newly acquired vegetable garden, she says matter-of-factly, "Naboth is dead." Notice that Ahab doesn't ask any questions; he doesn't care about details. He's thinking asparagus. He takes. His hands are clean. Archbishop Desmond Tutu, of South Africa, issued a memorable line in relation to the white regime's accountability for apartheid. He said, "It is very difficult to wake up someone who is pretending to be asleep." When I read this, I felt like he had named something that was going on inside of me.

I realize that I feel like I have been pretending to be asleep. My hands, like Ahab's, are clean, aren't they? I am not responsible for the injustices done to the indigenous people over the last 300 years, am I? Like Ahab, I don't really want too many details. I don't ask probing questions. I don't read books. I don't go out and listen to the court case in Nanaimo, although it's open to the public. I don't go to the Dialogue Series at Canadian Memorial Centre for Peace, at which native people are yearning for an audience. When a plea comes around for the Healing Fund of the United Church of Canada, I fold the letter back up and hope someone else will take care of these things. I am Ahab. I have simply and innocently taken what has been delivered to me. Furthermore, my church, which has always been on the side of Naboth, is now cast, in the media at least, in the role of King Ahab. We are receiving a wake-up call like never before in this province. We must stop pretending that we're asleep.

Yes, I know. It's more complex than it sounds. The lawyers representing the United Church of Canada are lawyers with the insurance company. We were not fighting with the victims, those natives who were abused. Our fight was with the feds over an equitable share of financial responsibility. From a legal point of view this was prudent. This is also why we have stopped short of an apology at General Council, and instead committed to a process of repentance. It was safer. It is indeed very complex, but Marion Best, our former moderator, remains profoundly regretful about what happened at that General Council. "I had hoped that the 36th General Council would have issued an apology. I know that there are many reasons why that did not happen, but I know we will never be reconciled until it does." (*Touchstone*, May 1998)

"Have you found me out, O my enemy?" This is Ahab's question to the prophet Elijah, who comes to deliver a different kind of news from that which Jezebel delivered to Ahab. Elijah has no goodies to deliver, only judgment. We too, are facing judgment, as the corporate body of Christ, and as individuals.

In situations of abuse, there are three stages of healing. First, the victim needs to tell his or her story, and be listened to. Second, he or she needs to hear from the perpetrator that he or she is not crazy, that these things did in fact happen. Third, there needs to be an apology and amends. We are just barely in Stage One in this nation. We have truly been found out. We must respond, not with guilt but with action.

There are hopeful signs. One of them is happening right here at Canadian Memorial. We are positioning ourselves to be facilitators in this healing process. There is a Sacred Circle workshop next Saturday, and in the fall we will be opening up the Dialogue Series to the wider public as it relates to land claims. We're getting calls from high-level native and government representatives who want the opportunity to be heard. We are not taking an ideological position on this but rather creating a neutral forum where the dialogue can be deepened, which can help to move us through all three stages of the healing process. There is no more pressing peace issue than our relationship with native people, and the reconciliation that needs to happen. We give God thanks for the witness of the United Church of Canada over the years. I am proud to be part of a church that is willing to be on the leading edge, even when that leading edge is defined by repentance and accountability. May God bless us as we open ourselves to the leading of the Great Spirit, and to the process of healing.

—June 14, 1998

Dying, We Find Life

JOHN 12:20-26

*"Unless a grain of wheat falls into the ground and dies, it
remains just a single grain; but if it dies, it bears much fruit."*

Once I lead a workshop at which I spoke about the need for
transformation. A crusty old professor was in attendance.
He made an immediate impression upon me, because the moment
I started speaking he would close his eyes. Well, this one time I
finished what I had to say and asked if there were any questions or
comments. He slowly began to open his eyes. This opening was a
process in and of itself, "sort of like a lizard," I thought to myself.
Then he spoke: "Have you ever considered that I might not want
to be transformed? I'm happy with the way I am, and I certainly
don't come to church to be transformed, or anything of the sort."
When he finished, he began the slow process of closing his eyes
again, sitting there motionless.

He has a point, I suppose. Some people spend their lives re-
making themselves. We all know workshop junkies who are on an
unending search for the key to unlock their full potential. There is
an earnest quality about these folks, who can be a bit obsessive.
But I rather doubt if the good professor had ever been to a workshop on personal growth. By far and away the greater problem
among human beings is not an earnest desire to evolve but rather
the refusal to do so.

How do we evolve spiritually as human beings? In the reading today, from John's gospel, Jesus describes how this happens. It is a great spiritual paradox. The disciples are having a hard time understanding what he is telling them about having to suffer and die, in order that all might be fulfilled. To help them understand he says, "Unless a seed falls into the ground and dies, it cannot multiply. Those who love their life in this world will lose it. But those who hate their life will keep it."

This is not an invitation to self-loathing. For most of us, self-loathing comes quite naturally. We can find all sorts of reasons to beat up on ourselves. But that's not what Jesus is talking about. He's alluding to something much more difficult, and spiritually challenging. Before any real growth is possible, a death is inevitable. Just as seeds need to undergo a death in order for the life to be released in them, so it is with all forms of life.

This is true on a planetary level. When the environment changed, a species had to die in one form in order to live in another. When the seas began to dry up, some life forms learned to live off of the land. Gills shrunk, lungs grew, fins became limbs, and new creatures evolved. It is no different for human beings. Johann Wolfgang von Goethe wrote a short poem describing this bio-spiritual truth:

Die and Become.
Till thou hast learned this
Thou art but a dull guest
On this dark planet.

The sleepy professor has become a metaphor in my consciousness that typifies the "dull guest." I learned the lesson through a dream. When I was 28 years old, I had a dream in which I was excited to be taking my new little puppy back to Winnipeg to show it to my family. I walked in the door, and the family dog, a big black Lab, jumped up and grabbed my little puppy by the throat and started to shake it. At that moment, I needed to make a decision. In order to save my puppy, it was clear that I would have to kill the family dog. I then choked the family dog to death, took my puppy and left, knowing that my family would not accept my choice. The puppy, of course, was the new life in me that I was being called to nurture. The family dog represented all the old loyalties and loves that would be threatened by my new life. It was clear that, in order for the new life in me to grow, I would have to die to an old self.

Unless a seed falls into the ground and dies, it cannot bear fruit. More often than not, genuine suffering is the soil in which a death of oneself occurs, so that a new life can flourish. Suffering can crack open the hard shell that we often confuse with the life within it.

We all have psychological shells that we think protect us and define us, but often they are merely prisons for the life within. A lot of us who are men live inside a shell that we confuse with who we really are, for example. Our shell requires that we act like men: don't express your need; don't be needy, period. Don't be soft. Always be in control emotionally. Be strong. It's not very often that we give ourselves permission to break out of the shell. The suffering that broke me out of the shell called "masculinity" was when my first marriage ended and my daughter went to live 1,500 miles away. My grief was so intense that I had to get to know this "me" who wept uncontrollably, who needed to be held and comforted, who was out of control. I do not regret this time of suffering. I died to an old self. When Jesus says that we should hate our lives, he is referring to that shell that we too often get so attached to that it becomes a tomb, rather than a womb for new growth.

The wedding day is an occasion in a young man's life when this shell called gender is cracked ever so slightly. I do a fair number of weddings, and I love to watch the groom, the best man, and the groomsmen in the twenty minutes or so before the wedding. They fix each other's corsages very carefully. They adjust each other's bow ties. They ask the groom how he's feeling, brush the lint from each other's pant legs. They tell each other how good they look in the tuxedo. They touch each other and deal with each other softly, for a change. For twenty minutes in their lives, they are so "not male." They have permission to engage in the intimate act of fussing over one another. It's really quite wonderful to see.

Lifestyle can be a shell that we fall in love with, confusing it with life itself and preventing our spiritual evolution. We are bombarded with images of the desirable lifestyle: these products, this style of home, this car, this look, this new real estate development, this golf club, these clothes. The package promises happiness. We can become so enamoured and therefore so focused on acquiring the package that in the process we lose our souls. Jesus' words are apt: "those who love their life in this world will lose it."

The success of Thomas Moore's book, *Care Of The Soul,* indicates that, although we still may be addicted to the pursuit of the perfect lifestyle, many are finding the whole enterprise empty. We are a culture in search of meaning. Moore recommends a return to simple things like writing longhand letters to friends, strolling each day in a garden, reading poetry, listening deeply to one's partner, cultivating the art of love, reflecting intellectually on what physicist Brian Swimme has called the "immensities," activities that take time and cannot be purchased. "Those who hate their lives in this world will find it." And again, what Jesus means is that we need to trust the inner voice of the soul, which finds materialism extremely unsatisfying. The spiritual life is about learning what death we need to suffer in order to have life.

Church, of course, is a shell that is in need of being continually cracked open, so that all the potential life within can be released to become all that God intended us to be. This breaking open always involves suffering. And we are in a period of suffering as a national church. Our struggle to acknowledge our complicity in the abuses of the Native Residential Schools is painful. One could hear it in the voice of our former moderator, Marion Best, who, because of legal counsel, stopped short of a full apology this past week at General Council. The apology, however, was in her quivering voice. We suffered greatly as a national church in 1988 and 1989. Other churches, although expressing great respect, think we're crazy for taking the lead on these issues. We are risking too much, they say. Perhaps. But if it is true that to save our life we must risk losing our life, then perhaps the key to our continuing spiritual evolution is this radical willingness to face our suffering when Reality requires it.

Those who follow Jesus cannot be dull guests on this planet. The way of the Christ is the way of ongoing evolution. He saw his own body as a shell and his own suffering as inevitable. But he knew the life within the seed could not but grow with God, despite his death. His death unleashed his spirit, and his spirit lives on in those who follow him. As Emily Dickinson has written:

A Death blow is a Life blow to Some
Who till they died, did not alive become—
Who had they lived, had died but when
They died, Vitality begun.

Friends, embrace your death and live.

—August 24, 1997

The Evolution of Communion

JOHN 6:52-65

"Those who eat my flesh and drink my blood have eternal life, and I will raise them up on the last day."

This morning, we get a glimpse into an early Christian community's struggle to understand the meaning of sharing bread and wine together, the sacred ritual we have come to call the sacrament of Holy Communion. Another name for it is "Eucharist," which is Greek for "Thanksgiving." Apparently, by the time John's gospel was written, this ritual was downright offensive for non-Christians and Christians alike. "How can this man give us his flesh to eat?" ask non-Christians (6:52). The followers of Jesus themselves admit, "This teaching is difficult; who can accept it?"(6:60). And we know from the Jewish historian, Josephus, that the Romans accused the Christians of being cannibals, of ritually eating the flesh of their leader, and drinking his blood.

Two thousand years later, I still find there is much confusion over what it is we are doing when we celebrate "communion." The first time I ever presided as an ordained minister at Holy Communion, a Roman Catholic priest who was present just about had a fit. I forgot to ask the Holy Spirit to change the bread and wine into the body and blood of Jesus Christ, and then when I was finished breaking the bread, I wiped the crumbs off onto the floor. I told him it shouldn't have mattered because I had failed in any case to turn the bread into Jesus. One could I say I had a rather low Eucharistic theology.

144

The Roots Of Communion

Communion is connected to three layers of tradition in the early church. At the first layer, it should not be surprising that the roots of communion go back to Jesus himself. Table fellowship or "open commensality" was Jesus' primary strategy for getting his message across about God's kingdom. This strategy was deceptively simple, radically undermining of the class structures of the Greco-Roman Empire and the purity codes of the Jewish faith.

Someone has said, "We are who we eat with." Jesus invited people who wouldn't normally find themselves at the same table to eat with each other: the impure, women, tax collectors, prostitutes. For this reason, he gained the reputation of being a glutton and drunkard. Jesus ate with people he wasn't supposed to eat with; through this practice of table fellowship, "walls that divide were broken down," to quote Strathdee's well-known hymn. When this motley crew sat together for a meal, what Jesus called the Kingdom of God was realized.

The first layer in the evolution of communion is a basic meal. Communion did not begin at the Last Supper. It began with Jesus' radical program of the open table. Communion is first and foremost a symbolic meal—realization of Jesus' vision for humanity.

Communion in Light of Jesus' Resurrection

The second layer of meaning flows from the early church's experience of Resurrection. After Jesus' death, the early church experienced that Jesus was somehow still present with them. This, of course, we call the Resurrection. Jesus' presence was particularly vivid when they got together to share a meal. It makes sense, doesn't it? How many times had the disciples experienced the power of Jesus' vision in the sharing of a meal? The story of the disciples on the road to Emmaus captures this experience most vividly. You'll remember that two disciples are walking back home after the crucifixion, when they are joined by a stranger. It's not until they sit down to break bread and share a meal of fish that they recognize that the stranger is the risen Christ. So, when we break bread and share the cup, we are doing a couple of things: first, we are remembering and reenacting the radical hospitality of Jesus of Nazareth; and second, we are celebrating the mystery of Christ's risen presence among us today. But symbols are multi-layered in their meaning, and so it gets more complex.

The third layer of meaning flows from the early church's attempt to make meaning of Jesus' death. And the primary meaning that was settled on was that it was a sacrificial death. The nature of that sacrifice has been debated and articulated through the ages. That's beyond the scope of this sermon. Suffice it to say that, at this point, the religion of Jesus became the religion about Jesus and his sacrifice. So the Eucharistic meal now begins to focus more on the sacrificial meaning of Jesus' death, and less on his radical program of the open table. For this reason, United Church people still tend to refer to an "altar" when in actuality it is for us a table.

When the early church began to experience significant growth, a full meal at every gathering became unrealistic. Bread and wine became symbols of the full meal. And the symbols themselves were understood to represent the body and blood of Jesus, broken and poured out for the forgiveness of sins.

The Last Supper

It is at this point that the tradition of the Last Supper crystallized. Jesus is recorded as instituting the Eucharist with the words, "This is my body, broken for you. This is my blood poured out for you." The story of the Last Supper is a ritual of the church. Most scholars doubt that it originated with Jesus himself. John's version is certainly not historical. You'll remember that John's was the last gospel written. In it, Jesus unabashedly refers to himself as God, as the Bread of Heaven, as the Bread of Eternal Life who surpasses the bread given to the Jews in the wilderness. They died, after all. But whoever eats of this Bread shall live forever. This is not Jesus speaking. It is the author of the gospel itself, who is locked in mortal battle with the Jewish synagogue and uses Jesus to assert the triumph of Christianity over Judaism.

Notice how we have now moved away from Jesus' strategy of the open table. The meaning has shifted dramatically toward Jesus' death as the sacrifice that gives us life, away from a strategy for social transformation of the outsider and towards a religious ritual for the insider's spiritual edification. Only the properly initiated, who share the same beliefs as we do, are welcome; children, of course, cannot take communion because they aren't really true believers yet.

The meaning has shifted away from a common meal and towards a religious sacrament needing an ordained priest who alone knows the secret language to change the bread into the body of Christ and the wine into Christ's blood; away from the table as symbol of community in which an alternative and radically egalitarian vision of Jesus is reenacted, towards an altar at which the ritual sacrifice is re-enacted. Around the altar a fence is constructed; we have the remnants of the fence here. The table is placed back away from the public, and begins naturally to assume a kind of spiritual aura, by virtue of the fact that only the mediator priests or ministers can rightfully approach it.

So, if you're confused about the meaning of communion, I'm not surprised. It is complex. I've talked about three layers of meaning: the historical layer which re-enacts Jesus' program of the open table; the Resurrection layer which celebrates Jesus continuing presence with us as we share a meal; and the meal as reenactment of Jesus' sacrifice which saves us from death.

I believe that it is time to shift the emphasis back toward the first two meanings so that it is more closely connected with Jesus' original vision. Originally, this table was simply that—a table—not an altar. It is an open table, at which we re-enact Jesus' ideal vision of God's kingdom, where all human beings are equal and welcome, regardless of economic status, gender, sexual orientation, race, or religion. There is nothing inherently sacred about a communion table. It takes on a sacred function insofar as it is where the Kingdom of God happens. I would say the same thing about the bread, the wine, the chalice. These are not sacred objects in and of themselves. We could make a communion table by throwing a three-quarter inch piece of plywood over a pool table, and serve the wine in tumblers. It's the openness of the table that makes it sacred.

I remember once in Israel being in a worship service of a different denomination, with people who had become our friends over the course of three weeks. We were gathered in the very place where St. Jerome had written the first Latin version of the Bible.

When it came time to receive communion, we were excluded because we didn't believe the same things that the people of this denomination believed. They imported a local male priest to serve. All the right prayers were said, the chalice was silver, the mood was very solemn, and for me it stood for everything Jesus was against. It was an experience of condemnation not salvation, of exclusion not inclusion.

It's time to reconnect this sacrament with the basic meaning that any child can understand. Either people are welcome at the table or they are not. They know the difference between being excluded and being included. This is the table of Jesus Christ. He breaks now all the artificial barriers we create, because he knows about the height and depth and breadth of God's love for humanity. He is the true host of this meal. When you receive the bread and wine, experience the love of Jesus Christ for you. Truly he poured himself out for all of us, gave us himself completely, that we might know the love of God. Eat, drink, and give thanks.

—August 17, 1997

From Aging to Sage-ing:
A Spirituality of Eldership

When Jungian analyst June Singer reached her 70th birthday, she entered into a profound spiritual struggle. Having moved through the life stages described by modern psychology, she entered a strange netherworld where there were no clearly marked stages. At this age, she thought, "One is supposed to be dead in the head. One isn't supposed to cause anybody any more trouble. As an old woman, you should take your place as a granny, utter an occasional wise statement, and get your hair fixed every week, so people will remark, 'But you don't look over 70!'"

In his book *From Aging to Sage-ing*, Rabbi Zalman Schachter-Shalomi reflects on Singer's experience of aging. "But Singer never bought into these cultural stereotypes. While on the surface things remained tranquil, her depths stirred with so many unanswered questions that often she found herself lying awake at night. During the day she sometimes drifted out of waking consciousness into a space of profound mystery where the unknowable cries out for attention."

Singer continues: "There are more and more elders like myself who have completed their allotted time and chores and who ask themselves, 'Why am I still here? To what purpose?' Stirring with passionate energy and concerns, we make space in our lives for embracing the spirit, refining the crucible of our self, and distilling its contents. In a time when the outer light begins to fade, we need to attend to the fire from within."

This morning marks the second worship service in two years focused on the theme of eldership. I must confess before going any further that neither last year nor this year have I particularly looked forward to preaching this Sunday. Partly, the reason is that I am in a different stage of my life. I am not elderly, although I know what it feels like to feel certain physical capacities waning. So I wonder what on earth I have to say or teach about eldership without being either patronizing or, even worse, conveying my own unconscious biases and fear around the aging process. Because, truth be told, there is a big part of me that sees the aging process as one long descent into the abyss of increasing dependence, decreasing mental and physical capacity, and greater risks of illness. Part of me doesn't trust this "fire within" theory that June Singer espouses.

You see, I am a product of our culture that is fixated on glorifying youth, one that values productivity and mastery above all. This culture, which has shaped my consciousness, informs me with a bias against growing old. From this way of thinking about aging, the fire within is slowly, inexorably, pathetically doused by time, and the last years before our ignoble exit from this world are a rather pathetic passage. From this perspective, to be an elder is to be taken care of; respect for elders is expressed by the habit of giving up one's seat on the bus to someone with grey hair, or opening a door for "them."

Both the culture that handed me this model and I are dead wrong, of course, and in the process of having to gather my thoughts for this service, I have been introduced to an alternative model or way of viewing our older years. I am grateful to Robert Raines and Rabbi Zalman Schachter-Shalomi for helping me to see anew. Let me share with you an experience I had while at Naramata Retreat Centre, teaching a course. While we were there, another group was meeting on the theme of healing our relationship with native people, led by a native man and a white woman. The group leaders would meet after our morning sessions and share our experiences. The white woman shared how she had made a very large mistake that morning. She was proceeding with her agenda, but one of the native woman elders decided to deliver a teaching, a very lengthy teaching, which was blowing the agenda for the morning to smithereens. The white leader intervened, and mentioned at one point that the group needed to move on. She was told in no uncertain terms by her native co-leader that she had displayed an enormous lack of respect for her elders. She would need to return the next day and apologize. The native culture has something to teach us about a different way of understanding what aging is about.

In that culture, old age does not mean just mean wrinkled skin and chronic disease. It means a growth into the wisdom, serenity, balanced judgment and self-knowledge that represent the fruit of long life experience. One of the readings this morning from John's gospel is a bit strange for this time of year, but I think it helps provide a context for the understanding of aging. The risen Jesus appears to Mary after his crucifixion, and she naturally reaches out to hold on to him when she realizes who it is. But Jesus prevents her, saying, "Do not cling to me, for I have not yet ascended to my Father." This is what is known in the Christian calendar as the ascension story. The understanding is that Mary and the disciples needed to let go of Jesus as they knew him, in order to receive the Holy Spirit and carry on the work of God.

There is no question that aging involves letting go of much that we have loved. Spouses and friends die before we are ready; we have to say good-bye to homes we have cherished; our physical health and mental capacities seem daily to abandon us; we have to let go of roles we have played in our careers and the domestic realm, or perhaps at church, that were meaningful. Without question, there is much grieving to be done in this process of growing older. The poet Robert Bly asked this question in a poem:

What is sorrow for? It is a storehouse,
set on Rocks, for wheat, barley, corn, and tears—
the storehouse feeds all the birds of sorrow . . .

Embracing sorrow is one of the tasks of aging. But that's not all there is. Mary was told by Jesus not to cling to him. He needed to go so that she could receive a new spirit. She wanted to cling to a particular age, but Jesus was trying to help her move into a new age, which required a new spirit. Something new was being born in her letting go, a new spirit for a new age.

And that is the task of aging, from a Christian perspective: receiving and living into the Spirit appropriate to this new age called eldership. And let's be clear; there is a difference between being elderly and eldership. Being elderly is what happens to us when we accept the cultural definition of aging. Being elderly is being old, pure and simple, a biological fact. It is largely a matter of putting in time, and being as pleasant as possible, until it's over.

Eldership, in contrast, is an active embracing of the possibilities inherent in aging. I am grateful to Rabbi Shachter-Shalomi for this distinction. Abraham Joshua Herschel penned the following words in a book called *The Insecurity of Freedom*: "One ought to enter old age the way one enters the senior year at a university, in exciting anticipation of consummation." Having spent a lifetime ascending the mountain, you now approach the summit, and from here you enjoy a panoramic perspective. Elderhood, then, is a state of consciousness that arises in the context of physiological aging, usually making its presence felt around the traditional retirement years, and following. At this time, the psyche issues a call for us to engage in life completion, a process that involves specific tasks such as coming to terms with our mortality, healing our relationships, enjoying our achievements, and leaving a legacy for the future. Elders who intentionally engage in this time of life become our sages. Aging becomes sage-ing.

For people who embrace active eldership, growing old is not necessarily a bad joke that God plays on us. By an act of faith they can say, "For the benefit of who we are, and who we may become, it's good to experience old age." It is a season of harvesting our lives, and offering the fruit of our being back to God, and thus becoming for the world a spiritual elder.

I have this vision of our elders turning to us in this congregation, and asking us the question that Jesus put to Peter: "Who do you say that I am?" Do we see our people of age as elderly? Or do we see you as potential elders? I imagine you asking us: "Do you see me as an old person who needs to be served and taken care of? Or do you see me as your elder who has wisdom, perspective and solid judgment to share with you?" Don't get me wrong. This is not a matter of doing more with your life; it's a matter of allowing the depths of your being to shine a light upon us—this community and this world.

I wonder further what would happen if we established a school of eldership at the Centre for Peace so that persons of age could get themselves into groups and engage the spiritual tasks of eldership with intentionality? Imagine the course description: Embracing Our Sorrow, Seeking and Offering Forgiveness, Celebrating our Lives, Harvesting Our Blessedness, Intimacy with God and

Others, Mentoring Our Young, Stewards of the Earth, Preparing to Meet Our Maker, Finding Our Prophetic Voice.

This morning we celebrate eldership. We celebrate the great gift of those of you who are in the zenith of your life, in the stage of fulfillment, approaching the summit with great wisdom and fullness of being to share with us. We give God thanks for you.

—September 17, 2000

Love of God, Love of Neighbour

MARK 12:28-34

"You shall love the Lord your God with all your heart, and with all your soul and with all your mind, and with all your strength, and you shall love your neighbour as yourself."

So a scribe comes forward, sees Jesus and the Pharisees arguing law, and chimes in: "Which of the commandments is the first of all?" If he were looking to trip Jesus up, a favourite sport of the religious academics, he would not have chosen this question. Every Jew, from the time he was old enough to speak, would have this one memorized. "Hear, O Israel, the Lord our God, the Lord is one; you shall love the Lord your God with all your heart and soul and mind and strength." Our Jewish friends call it the Shema. Orthodox Jews wear it on their forehead and put it over their doors. Love God with all that you are and all that you have. A no-brainer for any Jew worth his salt, and it is naturally Jesus' starting point.

But what does that mean, exactly? Right now, as I speak, Orthodox Jews are advocating all-out war on the Palestinian Arabs. I think the last count was 165 men, women, and children dead. I'm not going to go into the politics of the region, but suffice it to say that the Orthodox Jews who are advocating this bloodshed are doing it in faithfulness to the first commandment—loving God with all their hearts and souls and mind translates into killing the Arabs. The Islamic fundamentalists, for their part, may well be using

this very same first commandment to justify their call for an all-out *Ji-
had*, a holy war, against the Jews. Both leaders, Arafat and Barak, are
under tremendous pressure from the religious right to escalate the violence. The association between loving God and killing creates no
cognitive dissonance within the religious system that supports the violence. If you stop at the first commandment, it's possible to love
God and hate your neighbour. In fact, you can show your love of
God by hating your neighbour. Somehow it makes sense.

It stops making sense when Jesus carries on with the commandment that follows: "You shall love your neighbour as yourself." Now, loving God is inextricably connected with love of
neighbour. In fact, you can't have one without the other. If you
say you love God but hate your neighbour, you're breaking the
law. And you can't love your neighbour, especially if your neighbour is your enemy, without first loving God, which is what will
give you the wherewithal to love your enemy. With this second
commandment Jesus has just thrown a wrench into the gears.

And the scribe who put the question to Jesus knows it! We
know he gets it because of how he responds to Jesus' answer. Essentially he says, "You're absolutely right—these are the two most
important commandments." Then he says something which lets
us know that he really gets it, at gut level. He says: "These two are
more important than all whole burnt offerings and sacrifices."
And then, I imagine a deadly silence. You could hear a pin drop. It
reminds me of that REM song: "That's me in the corner, that's me
in the spotlight, losing my religion—Oh no, I've said too much."
Well, he said too much, and in doing so he was in the process of
losing his religion.

You see, you have to understand that the scribe has just undermined the entire religious system of his day. He has just said that
this second commandment basically supersedes sacrificial reli-

gion. The rivers of blood that flowed from slaughtered animals every day in the temple were expressions of the people's love of God. The religious institution of the day was the temple, and the temple was a monument to sacrificial theology. Everything was built out from around the Holy of Holies, the place where God was believed to dwell. In the Holy of Holies was an altar on which a whole bull would be sacrificed by the high priest, the only one allowed to enter, and only once a year. Of course, throughout the year there were daily sacrifices of animals as well, for various purposes, not the least of which was to feed the priesthood with what was left over. René Girard called it a system of sacred violence. Under this system, it is believed that the social and political order is maintained through proper ritualistic sacrifice.

When studying this story in Bible Study on Tuesday, we read the last line that says, "After that no one dared to ask him any questions." Kay Metheral immediately asked, "Why not? Why did no one dare to ask any more questions?" And the answer I want to suggest is that this scribe was led by Christ into coming to his own subversive conclusion—that all this killing of innocent animals had nothing to do with the essentials of faith in God. Christ was probably killed for this insight. No one really wanted to go there.

These animal sacrifices were part of a religious system that prophets from within the Jewish tradition itself condemned. The prophet Hosea said: "I desire steadfast love and not sacrifice, the knowledge of God rather than burnt offerings" (Hosea 6:6).

The prophet Micah asked the question, "With what shall I come before the Lord, and bow myself before God on high? Shall I come before Him with burnt offerings, with calves a year old? Will the Lord be pleased with thousands of burned rams? Shall I give my first born for my transgression, the fruit of my body for the sin of my soul?" No, but what the Lord does require of you is "to do justice, love kindness, and walk humbly" (Micah 6:6-8) In other words, love God by loving your neighbour. This was 800 years before Jesus was born.

Now I need to take you just a little way into sacrificial theology. Did you hear that line from Micah? Shall I give my first born for my transgression? This should chill us to the bone, because what is being referred to is human sacrifice. Animal sacrifice was very likely a substitute for human sacrifice. And human sacrifice, according to René Girard, was born of a very simple observation by early tribes. When violence broke out in the community or between two tribes, and it escalated to the extent that someone was killed, the violence ceased, as people gathered in hushed awe around the corpse. Peace was restored through a violent death. The death of the victim took on a kind of sacred aura. It had the power to restore order. Over time, rituals were developed in which there was an annual reenactment of this murder. Innocent victims were slaughtered in rituals of human sacrifice. The rituals proved to be cathartic, and they were believed to be the secret to political, social, and economic harmony. Religious ritual was sacrificial ritual, and the system of sacred violence was born.

The Bible tells the story of God moving in the Jewish people to break down this system of sacred violence, to disassociate love of God and violence. It was an evolutionary process. The first step was to stop human sacrifice, which is probably what the story of Abraham not sacrificing his son Isaac was about. The ram was substituted for a human sacrifice. The next step was for the prophets to condemn animal sacrifice. They believed that, if the community was governed by justice, compassion, and true humility, then the inherent violence of the sacrificial system would no longer be required to keep good order. Jesus' mission was to take humanity to the next step, which he called the Kingdom of God, in which all associations between love of God and violence in any form are severed. He lived for it, and he died for it. Christ responded to the ways of violence by taking it into himself; loving God and loving his neighbour meant enduring the desperate reassertion of the system of sacred violence. He was crucified.

The crucifixion of Christ exposed and undermined this system of sacred violence. All who witnessed it knew that Jesus was falsely accused and executed. It fooled no one. The soldiers who executed Jesus are reported as having confessed that surely he was God's son.

When we say God raised Christ up in the resurrection, we are really saying that violence will not have the last word. We are saying that Christ is alive, and what's scary is our claim that, wherever else Christ may be alive, he is certainly alive in us. We are the resurrected body of Christ, his flesh and blood in the world. Christ works in and through us, imperfect though we may be, to proclaim and enact a reign of peace on earth, to show the world that loving God and loving neighbour are inextricably linked.

This morning, All Saints' Day, we will end the service by singing "For All The Saints." I just want to mention four women, American nuns, who were murdered in El Salvador in 1980, by government troops to empower the poor. They are Maura Clarke, Jean Marie Donovan, Dorothy Hazel and Ita Ford. We give thanks to God for these women and for all the saints who loved God and loved their neighbour.

—November 5, 2000

The One Thing Lacking

MARK 10:13-27

When the rich man heard this, he was shocked and
went away grieving, for he had many possessions.

A man runs up to Jesus and kneels before him with a burning question. Have you ever been that earnest? I have. There was a period in my life when I would have prostrated myself on the path of anyone I thought could answer my questions about the meaning of life. Have you ever been this spiritually hungry? I mean, at those times my questions burned inside of me. Well, this man's question is one for the ages.

"Good teacher, what must I do to inherit eternal life?" Interesting question. I read once of a Chinese emperor who drank mercury thinking it was the secret of eternal life. It killed him eventually. People are serious about eternal life. Ernest Becker, a Pulitzer Prize-winning philosopher, developed a grand theory that all of human enterprise—the building of civilization, all industry, and our relationships—are formed around an unconscious but profound fear of our mortality. The fact that we die renders the whole deal downright meaningless, and so all human industry becomes an immortality project, a pursuit of eternal life. Hinduism calms humanity's fears about mortality with the doctrine of reincarnation. Evangelical Christianity deals with our fear of mortality with the claim that, by believing Jesus is God's only son, we get the assurance of eternal life. Every religion, including New Age religion, has to deal with the stark reality of death. ·

The man's question was one for the ages. He was prepared to do whatever he had to do to gain the prize of eternal life. "Good teacher," he begins, "what must I do to inherit eternal life?"

Jesus seems a little testy in response: "Why do you call me good? God alone is good." If this man thinks that one of the things he must do to inherit eternal life is butter up the teacher with a little flattery, he's got another think coming.

You see, doing good is this man's trump card. It's what he's depending on to gain eternal life. Jesus is teaching him a spiritual lesson here, but it's going to take a little fleshing out: "No one is good but God alone." Now, I don't believe that Jesus is stating some eternal truth about the sinful nature of humanity. Jesus is attempting to shift the man's thinking. If eternal life is a reward for being good, then Jesus excludes himself as a candidate. Good behaviour won't get the job done.

Remember the story of Job? Job was a good man; there was none better in fact. He was wealthy beyond measure, and everyone attributed it to his superior righteousness. It's the doctrine of meritocracy, that we get what we deserve, for good or for ill. If we've been good, we'll be blessed with prosperity and/or eternal life. The Book of Job was written to undermine this belief, but it was a persistent little devil. The rich man in our parable was banking on it, in fact.

He had worked all his life to be good. He has kept every one of the commandments since his youth. He tells this to Jesus. You almost get the sense that he's seeking some kind of assurance that, indeed, his good behaviour will be rewarded. The teacher has just found out about his good behaviour. Maybe he's passed the test. But then the hammer drops. A velvet hammer to be sure. Because, before Jesus challenges him, the writer of the gospel makes it clear that "Jesus loved him." Jesus feels immense compassion for this earnest man who has spent a lifetime doing good and is hoping against hope that it's enough for the big reward. Jesus loved the man.

"Just one thing," Jesus says to the man. "Go and sell all your possessions, give them away to the poor, and come and follow me." The man is "shocked." And who wouldn't be? All his possessions? The man walks away, the story says, "in grief." Jesus sees into this man's soul and asks him to do the one thing he knows he cannot do. With his money and his willpower there was nothing he could not do to gain eternal life. He could keep the commandments. He had enough wealth to pay his temple taxes and hire other people to slaughter his animals so he would remain ritually pure enough to earn eternal life. But Jesus finds the one thing he cannot, by his own power, accomplish.

Have you ever reached that limit? When you come to the realization that you don't have what it takes? I have felt that as a minister, many times. You work like a madman and lie in bed at night exhausted, knowing you've given it all you've got and more, but it's still not enough. All you can think of is what's not done, and whom you haven't called, why so-and-so never came back to church. And at that moment, you know the grief in that man's heart as he walks away, realizing he hasn't got what it takes.

But do you know what I think? I think Jesus intended this man's grief to be the beginning of a conversation about the spiritual life, not the end. And I think that if I could only learn in those moments of desperation when I've reached my limits, that Christ is there asking: "Well, what are you depending on? Your own ingenuity, your own energy, your notions about what you think is possible?"

I know this man who walked away in grief. I know, too, he

should have stuck around. Notice that Jesus didn't send him away. He walked away himself. He missed an opportunity for conversion. He was this close to the Kingdom of God. Because I think if he had stuck around and confessed that he'd done all that he could do, and this was simply too much, then he could have fallen on his knees before Christ and experienced the one thing that could really have saved him—the love that Jesus had in his heart for him. A love that would have just held him in his pain and grief, and whispered in his ear, "You don't have to do anything to get this love." He walked away, when all he needed to do was receive it.

In the verses preceding this story, Jesus takes the children up in his arms and blesses them. Children! They didn't do a blessed thing. But Jesus touches them and says what? "Whoever does not receive the Kingdom of God as a little child will not enter it."

The children have the one thing the rich man lacks: radical dependence on grace. Religion would have you believe it's all about doing good, and achieving eternal life. Spirituality, true spirituality, is not about doing or achieving at all. It's first and foremost about receiving. You know, Jesus wasn't really very interested in life after death. He didn't talk about it much. He probably simply assumed that, like life itself, it is just one more gift from God. He certainly didn't think it was a prize for moral perfection here on earth. What he did talk about was the Kingdom of God. Did you notice how the man wanted to talk about eternal life, but Jesus wanted to talk about the Kingdom of God?

"How hard it is for the wealthy to enter the Kingdom of God. It's easier for a camel to pass through the eye of a needle than for a rich man to enter the Kingdom of God." If you're wealthy, you can get to a place where you never really have to receive anything from anyone else, including God. You don't need anything. And when you don't need anything, it's real easy to forget that life is a gift. Life is what you've created for yourself and your family.

The Kingdom of God begins with the awareness that everything I have and everything I am, and everything that is, is a gift of love from God. We don't have to do anything except show up. And at every moment in every circumstance, God wants to provide all that we need. Eternal life? Well, that's a mystery you'll have to wait a lifetime to find out about. The Kingdom of God? You can walk through the doors, right now. All it takes to enter is a letting go of our tight-fisted attachment to our power, our ingenuity, our wealth, our families, our goodness, as if any of these represents something we've achieved, as if they represent anything but God's gracious gift to us. All it takes to enter is to open our hands, to let go, and offer it all back to the One from whom all blessings flow. All it takes is to follow Jesus back into the heart of God.

—*October 15, 2000*

Reading The Bible: Why Bother?

NEHEMIAH 8

Ezra opened the book in the sight of all the people, and when he opened it all the people stood up . . . For all the people wept when they heard the words of the law.

When the people of Israel heard their Scriptures read to them after years of doing without, they wept. What are we to make of this library of books, poetry, letters, Psalms, and history we call the Bible? Fundamentalists assure us that every word in the Bible is from the mouth of God. Some feminists are convinced that the Bible has outlived its usefulness, and that it has hurt the cause of women's equality. But every Sunday, we stand and sing as the Bible is brought forward, following in the Protestant tradition of giving it a central place in worship and in the living of our lives. Indeed, when I was interviewed for this position, I made it clear that Biblical literacy was among my highest priorities. This morning, I want to talk about why we should bother to read the Bible. My bias is that reading the Scripture is still life-giving.

But let's be honest. The Bible is not an easy library of literature to get through. It was written and compiled in a world so very different from our own. There are customs, rituals, and cultural assumptions that are difficult to relate to. Even the way it portrays God is hard to swallow sometimes.

As you heard from David Kennedy last week, 22 people read

through virtually the entire Bible over a period of 34 weeks. This required a commitment of somewhere between five and eight hours per week per person. As a leader, I found the experience fascinating and rewarding. Halfway through the First Testament, we began to notice a widespread lament. Summarized, the lament sounded something like this:

"Why are we bothering to read this? There is so much violence, murder, deceit, and outdated notions about diet and purity laws. I don't even like the God that is portrayed much. He's a tyrant! He sanctions violence! He's a He!"

This was challenging for me as a leader. We had built the program up, after all, as an opportunity for spiritual edification. It made me realize that, to be honest about it, there are some very real hurdles to clear. Anyone of these can trip you up and make you feel like quitting the race. I want to spend a few minutes talking about these hurdles because they do trip up people.

Hurdle #1: A Different Cosmology

The Bible is written from a pre-scientific cosmology or worldview. It was a three-tiered Universe: in the middle was the earth, up above were the heavens, and the dividing line was the blue dome we know as the sky. At night there were little pinpricks in the dome, which revealed the heavens beyond…these are the stars. Underneath was the third tier, Sheol, or the underworld. Ever since the first astronauts looked back on earth from outer space, this worldview is gone forever. There is no up and no down. There is no "outside" in this Universe. Furthermore, the Bible knows nothing about evolution. In short, our cosmology or worldview is vastly different from the Biblical worldview.

Hurdle #2: Patriarchal Assumptions

The Bible is written from a patriarchal worldview. For many feminists, this is reason enough to dismiss the Bible. Women are clearly second-class citizens. In the story of Lot, for example, in Genesis, when the inhabitants of the city of Sodom demand Lot's male guests so that they can rape them, Lot instead offers up his two daughters. Phyllis Tribble, a feminist theologian, calls these stories "texts of terror" from the point of view of women, and her view cannot be easily dismissed. In most of the Bible, women are clearly not equal to men. The Bible was written from a patriarchal worldview. There is much in it that is not kind to women.

Hurdle #3: The Image of God

The third hurdle has to do with the portrayal of God. Because the socio-political context of the era in which most of the Bible was written was patriarchal, God is portrayed as the dominant patriarch of the universe. God is predominantly male, and presented naturally as the epitome of the male power figure: Lord and King, like an Egyptian Pharaoh, for example, except with more power to make things go exactly as he pleases than even those power figures had. In much of the Bible, God is portrayed as monarch, lawgiver, and judge who punishes with death when these laws are broken.

Hurdle #4: A Tribal God

Finally, a fourth hurdle is this: The God of much of the Bible is a tribal god; the tribe is the Hebrews or the Israelites. They are one small tribe among many in the Mideast, literally fighting for their survival and a piece of land to call home. These Hebrews were semi-nomadic; they were slaves in Egypt for hundreds of years, and in order to survive they needed a god who was more powerful than all the other surrounding tribal gods. Their god was a tribal warrior god. And one of the distinguishing features of the Hebrew god was that he was a more powerful warrior. As a warrior god, he is portrayed as either sanctioning or directly effecting the slaughter of thousands and thousands of other men, women, and children in a battle for territorial supremacy.

These are significant hurdles, and there is no use denying their existence. So, why on earth read the Bible? If God is patriarchal, tribal, a warrior and a stern lawgiver, if the cosmology is so vastly different from our own, why bother? Some might contend: "Well, you're just talking about the Old Testament. The New Testament is different."

Not so fast. The New Testament also was written from the context of patriarchy. Remember: Paul, the earliest Christian writer, continues to silence women in church, requires that they cover their heads and be submissive to men. He does not question the institution of slavery. What is distinct, of course, about the New (or Second) Testament is this man named Jesus of Nazareth, whom we call Christ, the anointed one, the one who heals the world. But let's be careful here as well. Let's not make the assumption that in Jesus there was an abrupt and totally new revelation, which came out of the blue, rendering the revelation of the First (or Old) Testament obsolete. For too many years, Christians have thought like this and therefore have perpetuated a triumphalist, "We're better than you," anti-Semitic and anti-Jewish attitude.

The Second Testament is centred on Jesus, stories about his life, his death, and his resurrection, and reflections on the meaning of this revelation for our own lives. But understand this: You will search in vain to find anything radically new in the teachings of Jesus, or the stories about Jesus, that you wouldn't find in the First Testament. The fundamental claim that is new is that this Jesus is the long-awaited Messiah. Beyond that, it was all in the First Testament. Jesus crystallizes and embodies the presence of God, which is witnessed to in the First Testament.

Why bother reading the Bible? Because, the real surprise for me is that, despite the patriarchal worldview, despite Yahweh being portrayed as a tribal warrior, despite all of this, the one we call "God" actually manages to find a way to shine through. The Bible, in other words, reveals God. This is a remarkable statement. I have always believed it with my head because, after all, it was called the "word of God." But reading through the Bible in depth for the last 34 weeks, I actually experienced a Holy Presence shining through.

René Girard calls the Bible a "text in travail." In other words, Something or Someone is trying to be birthed in and through this record of God's relationship over time with the Jews. It's like the mystery we call God is saying to these people, the Jews: "Work with me here." It is a painful labour that God goes through, but for those who persevere, the birth of God happens in and through these stories. There is a slow, sometimes painful dawning of consciousness in the community of faith, about the nature of God, and about what God requires. That dawning of awareness emerges in a crucible of a sacred covenant, a promise that God wouldn't give up on these people, no matter how long it took, if they would just stay open. Let's trace some of the breakthrough revelations which stretched God's people over time to incorporate a bigger, less parochial, and more compassionate God.

Blessed Are The Poor

In a world in which the powerful and dominant are believed to be divinely blessed, and the poor and downtrodden to be cursed, the revelation of Scripture reverses this: The Bible over and over affirms that God is with the victims of the powerful and dominant. There is a preferential option for the poor and dispossessed throughout the Bible. When the Jews forgot this in periods of prosperity, prophets were raised up—like Amos, Hosea, and Micah—to forcefully remind them. The Beatitudes, in which Jesus says, "Blessed are the poor," crystallizes the emergent revelation. It is not too strong to say that our modern-day assumption that the victim has rights that need to be honoured is a gift from Scripture. This is the witness of God's people.

Living Sacrifices

In a world in which sacrificial violence was the norm, this God manages to get the message through that this is not the sacred way. Abraham is about to sacrifice his own son Isaac, but at the last moment God intervenes to save Isaac. The message? God says to God's people, "These other surrounding tribal gods demand human sacrifice, but it is against my nature." So the Jews replace human sacrifice with animal sacrifice. We think of animal sacrifice as brutal, and it is, but understood against the background of human sacrifice, we should think of it as a moment of spiritual evolution for humanity.

Even animal sacrifice is criticized in the First Testament as a way to appease God. "I hate, I despise your burnt offerings," says God in Hosea. There is an evolution away from human and ani-mal sacrifice, in favour of understanding our entire living, our lives, as the sacrificial offering that pleases God.

Incidentally, it is also why the dominant Christian understand-ing of Jesus' death as a sacrifice, which God required to save us from sin, is a massive *devolution*. It is certainly how much of the New Testament makes sense of Jesus' death, but it runs contrary to the more evolved revelation of Scripture, and we need to retire it. Jesus' whole life was a sacrificial offering inspired, not required, by God. His death was a brutal execution, and not the will of God. It was also not the end of God. In the resurrection, God's way of peace triumphs. This is the witness of God's people.

Called For Service

Whenever God's people in the Bible start to think that they enjoy a position of privilege, God rudely awakens them to the fact that they are chosen for service, not privilege. They are chosen to be a light to the world. This does not give them the right to make triumphalistic assumptions about being the only ones God chooses. God forced Jonah, the reluctant prophet, to go to the Ninevites, the enemies of the Jews, to preach a message of repentance to them, thereby including them among God's people. Jonah represents that aspect of the Jewish and Christian communities that have a far more exclusivist understanding of God, namely, God is our God; we are holy, they are unclean; we have truth, they do not. In Jesus of Nazareth, this message of Jonah is radicalized; he tells parable after parable about how God loves the Gentiles, and how the Gentiles are more faithful than his own people. That is why any Christian denomination that declares the Christian faith as the only faith, the only way to be saved, and that others are able to get in only by believing what Christians believe about God, is anathema to the way of the Christ. We have no privileged status with God. God's people are those who have understood that they have been chosen for service, not for special status with God. This is the witness of God's people.

The Evolution of God

Finally, the image of God evolves as the sacred story develops. Or rather, it dawns on the covenant people that their image of God is way too small. When Moses experiences God in a burning bush and wants to know God's name, God says, "Tell them that 'I am' has sent you, or 'I will be who I will be'." The point is that God will not be domesticated. God refuses to fit neatly into our social, cultural, and political agendas. God's image evolves over time from warrior, harsh judge and lawgiver who loves us only if we are good, to "Daddy," whose love sends us out before we've done one blessed thing right, and inspires us to do the right thing. And so the religious life is not about behaving properly because of some great cosmic threat of judgment. It's about experiencing God's love, being transformed by that love, and living accordingly. This was the revelation that totally transformed St. Paul. It dawns on the community of faith that the fundamental characteristic of God is not warrior, not judge or lawgiver, but compassionate lover. Ultimately, anything that gets in the way of compassion, including religion, is not of God.

There are seeds of revelation scattered throughout Scripture. They are intended to take hold in the rich soil of our soul, and thrive. The weed that chokes the growth of this revelation is Biblical literalism; it is the wide sweep of the Biblical epic, not isolated verses, that reveals God. The shallow soil that prevents the revelation from growing roots and taking hold in our lives is not knowing the story of our faith. The birds that come along and snatch the seed before it ever has a chance are the many distractions of life that cause us to say, "I just don't have time to read the Bible."

But if we take the time to read the Bible, the seed will take root and rise in our very being. The witness of God's people is that, when we wrestle with Scripture, play with it, reflect on its meaning for our own lives, it mediates the presence of a living God. God sneaks off the pages of Scripture and into our lives, and becomes real for us. This is why we should bother with the Bible.

—*June 7, 1998*

Scars and All

ACTS 3:12-19; LUKE 24:36-48

"Look at my hands and my feet; see that it is I myself."

In 1989 my wife, Ann, and I took a three-week trip to Israel. It was a profound experience for both us. To be honest, I never really expected it to be so meaningful. I thought it would be a solid academic experience, because we were taking two courses while we were there. But only a couple of days after arriving, I realized that this was going to be much more than an intellectual exercise. It became an emotional and spiritual pilgrimage. The whole business of walking where Jesus walked, standing in the places he taught, walking through the streets of the villages and cities where he healed, was moving. Jesus became much more real to me. I experienced Jesus as my rabbi. So this Easter, when we read the story of the risen Jesus appearing to Mary at the tomb, and she exclaims "Rabboni!" which means teacher, I identify with her at an emotional level.

"What is it about Jesus that we cannot live without?" A colleague of mine once asked me this question. Notice that to answer it requires more than an intellectual response. It hits you at an emotional level. It doesn't ask which doctrine of the church you cannot live without. To answer it requires a disclosure of passionate intensity. Can't live without Jesus? Another way of asking this is, "How is Jesus your lifeline?" At this point, faith gets personal. I'm re-reading a book called *Sophie's World*. It's about a 14-year-old girl being introduced to the history of philosophy by a mysterious, unnamed teacher. At one point, he sends her a video of the ruins of ancient Athens, where Socrates and Plato once taught. And then something magical happens. She's watching the video, and suddenly she's face to face with the real Socrates. At that moment this is no longer ancient history. Now it's personal.

If Jesus is just an ancient historical figure we talk about, then our faith is somewhat of an intellectual exercise. Rather, we need to experience him in some personal, life-changing way. Let's take a look at Luke's story in this morning's reading. The risen Christ appears to the disciples, but they don't believe it any more than you or I would believe it if it happened to us. They think it must be a ghost, but Jesus assures them he is no ghost. This man who is picking the bones out of his fish so he doesn't choke on them is the same one who died three days ago. That's what Luke wants to get across to us. To put it theologically, the Easter Christ is the Good Friday Jesus, scars and all. He shows them his hands and his feet, where the Roman spikes went in and held up his crucified body. Luke is saying, in rather dramatic fashion, that there is no Christ, and therefore no Christianity apart from this Jesus of Nazareth, Galilean peasant. To be a Christian is to know Jesus of Nazareth.

Why does this matter? Well, in many ways, first-century Mediterranean culture was very similar to our own. It was a Hellenistic culture, characterized by hundreds of schools of Greek philosophy, mystery cults, and all kinds of religions. Israel was the centre of three or four empires, and so religion was an eclectic mix of Egyptian, Greek, Roman, and Assyrian thought. It was a veritable potpourri of spirituality. Two thousand years later, we face a similar phenomenon. There is unprecedented interest in, and varieties of, spirituality. This is especially true in a west coast city like Vancouver. It's really quite wonderful and rich. There has never been more interest in God.

But what is this God like? Well, for us when we're talking about God, we're not just referring to some kind of spiritual energy, or cosmic vibration, or harmonious feeling. We're talking about the God who, for us, in human form was fully present in Jesus of Nazareth. Now, listen, I'm sure the God of this universe comes in many shapes and forms, but to the church this God is grounded in the historical person of Jesus of Nazareth. That same Jesus is alive in the church, and more radically as the church, because what is the church if not people like you and me who have put him at the centre of our lives?

Luke reminds us that if the Jesus who died belongs to the historical past but the one disciples now follow is the eternal Christ, then the Christian life can take on forms of spirituality that have nothing to do with the teacher, prophet, egalitarian, social prophet, or healer we find in the gospels. No, Jesus is our compass, our grounding, our window on God. There is absolutely nothing wrong or nothing evil about other forms of spirituality. It's just that, for us, Jesus is the starting point, the compass, and what for us is the authentic measure of what it means to be fully human. It's time in the life of our church to return to Jesus in a radical way.

Have you noticed the renewed interest in Jesus of Nazareth? This year alone I've read books by three New Testament scholars: Burton Mack, John Crossan, and Marcus Borg. They represent a very small sample of intense research that is going on around Jesus. Some Christians find their research very unsettling; some dismiss it as unnecessary meddling in orthodox truths. As for me, I regard it as a movement of the Holy Spirit.

There is growing within me a vision of mainline congregations like ours developing a radical evangelism. Is this an oxymoron? Mainline evangelism? Here's how I see it happening. I see the laity gathering in groups to really get into the Bible, particularly with a view to knowing Jesus. Alongside the Bible, there will be stacks of books by the Jesus scholars. We will learn about first-century Mediterranean culture, Judaism in the time of Jesus, Roman law and culture. And as we do, it will dawn us with the same power as it dawned on the first disciples, just what this man was about. We will get excited like the first disciples and appreciate in a fresh way that Jesus has the power to save, or if that word has been tainted for you, as it has been for me, he has the power to heal humanity. We'll be moved to rededicate our lives as disciples of Jesus and be witnesses in the world. Yes, folks, I'm talking about mainline evangelism.

But this is evangelism with a difference. For one thing, it will be open and inclusive, deeply respectful of other religious traditions and forms of spirituality, but not afraid of promoting our own convictions. For another, it will be an evangelism that is based on the conviction that God's love is persuasive not coercive. We will not issue threats of eternal condemnation for those who believe differently from what we believe.

But we will claim that, in Jesus Christ we are a new creation, and there is life in abundance. We will approach the Bible not as the literal word of God but as the authentic memory of God's people. Occasionally, as in the reading from the Acts of the Apostles this morning, a reading reflects not the Spirit of God as revealed by Jesus of Nazareth but the politics of the writer. When this is the case, we will set the reading in context.

Finally, it will be an evangelism that will lift up the poor and oppressed in Jesus' name, and that find its most mature expression in service of others. We will always remember that, when Jesus appeared to the disciples after his death, he showed them his hands and feet; his credibility was based in his scars, signs of his willingness to suffer so that others may have life.

Jesus' final directive to the disciples is interesting. They are told to wait in Jerusalem until they are "clothed with power from on high." Jesus tells them to wait for power before doing any mission. I believe that, as we approach the 21st century, this is something Jesus might well tell the mainline churches as well. This is a waiting time. Not a passive waiting but an active waiting. We are waiting for power. For Luke, this power came from the Holy Spirit.

For us, I think the waiting will be around spiritual formation. I think we need a time to learn the Biblical story, to learn how to pray, to recharge our spiritual batteries in vibrant, dynamic worship services, to train our laity for ministry. Until we have dramatically reoriented ourselves around Jesus, around prayer and Biblical knowledge, our witness will lack power. Our new Centre for Peace should be regarded as a centre of learning, what Jews call synagogue, where adult learning, faith development, and the discernment and development of spiritual gifts for ministry takes place.

Listen: by the grace of Jesus Christ, and in the power of the Holy Spirit, there is no reason to lament the future of the church. Let us turn to this Jesus, in whom the fullness of God dwells, and in his name spread the love and compassion of God to our community. Amen.

—April 13, 1997

The Seat of Glory

MARK 10:35-45; HEBREWS 5:1-10

*"Are you able to drink the cup that I drink, or be baptized
with the baptism that I am baptized with?"*

T his past week, I was reading some articles about leadership,
and came across some analysis of John DeLorean, who
some of you may remember as a man who worked for General
Motors and then jumped ship to create his own car company. The
company ultimately failed, and the author of the article I read attributed it to his style of leadership. One executive of the
DeLorean Motor Company, after being dismissed by DeLorean
from the company board, commented: "He told me he knew that
some of the things the Board was doing bothered my conscience
and not to worry as much as I did, so he dropped me from the
Board. When I told him he couldn't bear having someone disagree
with him so he had to stack the Board his own way, John just nod-
ded and said, 'That's right. It's my company, and I'm going to do
what I want to do; when you get your own company, you can do
the same. You're fired'."

Jesus said, "You know that among the Gentiles those whom
they recognize as their leaders lord it over them, and their great
ones are tyrants over them." (Mark 10:42)

Jesus is doing a little leadership training here, folks. You see, Jesus
had a vision from the get-go. He called it the Kingdom of God, or
the commonwealth of God. The Kingdom was not some far-off-

in-the-future fantasy, nor was it something you had to wait to experience in the next life. It is what life looks like when you radically trust God. It's what happens between human beings when they lead with their heart and not their egos. It's a here-and-now reality that you enter when the poor are lifted up and the rich are brought down to eye level with them. It's what happens when we let God be God. Because when we do, we can understand that we are here to serve, not to be served. That was the vision.

He also had a strategy. And a large part of that strategy was choosing a group of ordinary people who would go into training around teaching about the Kingdom of God, and then enable others to dwell in that sacred space and time. So for three years he worked with his disciples, lived and ate with them day in and day out, grooming them for the day that he would leave them and they would have to carry on. A big part of Jesus' strategy was the cultivation of spiritual leaders.

I don't know when the church moved away from Jesus' strategy, but somewhere along the line, church became a matter of trying to take care of the needs of congregations, both pastoral and educational. There is nothing wrong with this, but notice that when Jesus gathered those first disciples, it wasn't about taking care of them, and it wasn't even primarily about their own spiritual growth. I'm sure they loved each other and cared for each other, and that they grew spiritually in the presence of Jesus. But these were not ends in themselves. They were means to an end. And the end was becoming spiritual leaders, so that they could help people to enter the Kingdom of God.

What I'm discovering the longer I'm in ministry is that the pews are filled every Sunday morning with potential spiritual leaders capable of delivering Jesus' vision. A great renaissance is happening in the church because we are starting to tap into this potential. We're beginning to realize that the job of our laity is not to manage the church. You're not volunteers who run the church. You are spiritual leaders who are the church. In the fourth century, when Constantine made Christianity the official religion of the Empire, he started to build churches. This was a foreign concept to Christians for 300 years. They had always met in people's homes or out in fields, and now there were church buildings to meet in. Prior to this, "the church" was not a building; it was a movement, a community living into and out of the Kingdom of God.

So the church became identified with a building, which needed some professionals to run it; these were called the clergy, and the clergy needed helpers, and this became the role of the laity, to help out at "the church," now a physical building that needed to be managed and maintained. You can't believe the number of churches, 1,700 years later, for whom this has become the mission—the maintenance and management of the church. It's a lot different from Jesus' mission and strategy of raising up spiritual leaders out of ordinary men and women.

Not that this was easy. Some days, it must have been quite a stretch for Jesus to hold onto his vision of the disciples as potential spiritual leaders. This was not exactly a banner day for Jesus. He has just finished announcing that he will be handed over to the authorities; flogged, humiliated, and then murdered, and on the third day be "raised up."

Well the sons of thunder, James and John, hear this and apparently all they can think about is positioning themselves for the seat of honour when Jesus comes into his glory. It reads like a modern-day political story. This is backroom politics. You'd think they'd have a little compassion, but no, they're calculating. They call a clandestine meeting with their leader, and say, "Teacher, we want you to do for us whatever we ask of you. Grant us to sit, one at your right hand and one at your left, in your glory."

Now it's possible to give them the benefit of the doubt here and posit that their motives are honourable, that they simply want to be close to their Teacher, in life, in death, and in the life to come. But judging by the reaction of the other disciples, I think we can rule this out. "They began to be angry." They saw it for what it was: a brazen case of secretly lobbying the Lord, looking out for Number One in glory land.

This is the kind of stuff that drives your friends who don't go to church crazy. They imagine that church, of all places, should be free of politics and power plays. And the moment they get the first whiff of it, they're gone. Well, Jesus had to deal with it, and the church will have to deal with it for as long as the church is around, because human beings inside the church are works in progress, just like our friends outside the church.

Actually, I find the candour of James and John rather refreshing. Typically, those who want power and status within congregations are a lot subtler. I have yet to have anyone come up to me in 15 years of ministry and say, "Hey, listen Bruce, I would like to be Chair of the Board so that I can throw my weight around a bit. Could you pull a few strings and make it happen?" I mean, I could deal with that! It's times when the person is unaware himself or herself that he or she is driven by ego gratification that we're in real trouble. Sometimes, of course, it's the minister who has a low self-image, or at an unconscious level feels inferior, and compensates by abusing his or her power in the congregation.

The point is that we have all sinned and fallen short of the glory of God, like James and John. But the acid test of whether one's heart is centred in God is whether you're willing to be to be a servant.

Narcissistic personalities are incapable of servanthood. Bill Hybels, from Willow Creek Church in Chicago, often takes the senior-executive big shots in his church away on retreat. Once, a CEO with United Airlines joined a retreat and the first thing Bill did was to give him menial tasks to do. He asked him if he would mind going to his car to get some papers Bill had left behind; then he asked him if he'd mind cleaning the bathroom. You see, this weekend was for leaders of the church, and Bill was checking out whether this man had the heart of a spiritual leader. His credentials as a leader in the world were impeccable, but spiritual leadership requires a whole different résumé.

Jesus looks at James and John after their pitch for power—"Can we sit at your right hand and at your left hand when you come into glory?"—and says: "You do not know what you are asking." Because if you're going to sit with me in my glory, you're also going to have to die with me on the cross. If you're willing to die to the part of you, James and John, that caused you to ask that question, then truly you are able to drink the cup that I drink, and truly you will know the meaning of my baptism and yours.

We're not perfect in the church, not by a long shot, but we know enough about sin working through our egos that we understand the need to be in prayer, to be in worship, to be with a trusted group of disciples who aren't fooled by the subtleties of ego. And I know enough about this congregation to know that these pews are filled with servant leaders, who are willing to drink the cup that Christ drinks, and be baptized into his death, so that we can be raised up, new creations, spiritual leaders in and for this world that God loves so much.

—*October 22, 2000*

The Sins of Our Fathers
On the Occasion of the Montreal Massacre

ISAIAH 11:1-10; MATTHEW 3:1-12

"They shall not hurt or destroy on all my holy mountain,
for the earth will be full of the knowledge of the Lord."

On Thursday I wrote one sermon. On Friday I wrote this one. In the first, I alluded to the horror of the massacre of 14 women in Montreal. I realized that a passing allusion to a tragedy of such proportions was unconscionable. This sermon addresses the horror of those murders.

This will not be easy to hear. There is, in all of us, including me, a built-in denial, when it comes to letting in atrocity. I wrote the first sermon on Thursday, even though I was fully aware of the massacre on Wednesday night. My denial was strong. I believe this sermon will be particularly difficult for the men here this morning. What I have to say invites you to extend and stretch. I invite your openness, and your reflections in the coming weeks.

On Thursday evening, men and women gathered together at Victoria University around a sculpture of a crucified woman, hanging naked and exposed, arms outstretched. They wept, they raged, they comforted each other, as the shock of the massacre deepened into powerful feelings.

Audrey McLaughlin, leader of the New Democratic Party, puts words to our own grief:

Those lost lives were our future: young minds who were attending school to acquire an education to work in their community, to share their abilities with their friends and families; young minds who wanted to contribute to Canada; and, I guess, young hearts who wanted to love.

Before we analyze, before we try to wring any meaning out of these killings, before we learn any lessons, we can only fall silent in grief for the loss of these 14 women, and before the unimaginable pain of mothers and fathers, and sisters and brothers.

The voice of the young male killer is heard saying these words before the premeditated slaughter: "You're women, you're going to be engineers. You're a bunch of feminists!"

There can be no question in anyone's mind about one fact—these killings were a social and political statement. At the end of the shooting, 14 women were dead for one reason: they were women. Their male classmates are alive for one reason: they are men. Yes, this atrocity was perpetrated by a very sick man. No question about it. But the question that begs to be asked is the one that served as the headline for a *Globe and Mail* editorial, "Why were women in the gunsight?"

We want to believe that this is simply a random act of a maniac. Period. Over and done with. We don't really want to go further and ask if at another level this massacre serves as a grotesque symbol for a dark and hidden reality in our society. Men's violence against women is crystallized in the gruesome event. It's also a symbol of men's confusion as women begin to occupy professions traditionally the exclusive domain of men. We do know, for example, that the killer, Marc Lepine, was taking night courses to try to get into l'École Polytechnique, where the women were killed. These killings break through our denial, and galvanize evidence and statistics that we've given only passing notice to up to this point.

On Thursday night, one young woman at a vigil in Montreal looked into the TV camera and told the nation: "Look, I've just come from a shelter for battered women, where I work. The shelter is full—full of women whose bones have been crushed, and self-esteem ravaged by their husbands." In 1983, Toronto had three shelters for battered women. Today there are 11.

And there are a lot more than 14 women beaten, raped, and sometimes killed, every week in this city. Approximately 80% of women murdered in Canada are murdered by men. In the last 15 years, Ted Bundy murdered 36 women. Edward Jackson, church-goer, respected doctor and father, raped 32 women. Christopher Thomas killed ten women and children in Brooklyn. In Canada, Larry Takahashi raped 14 women in Edmonton, between 1979 and 1983. Kenneth Steingard of Winnipeg killed his former girl-friend, his cousin's wife, and their two children. Six Brampton youths gang-raped a 14-year-old girl. Dianna Russell, a lecturer at Mills College in California, expert on violence, summarizes her 20 years of research with these words: "Violence is a male thing, and it's spreading."

This is not easy to hear, I realize. As I take all this in, part of me wants to scream in protest, "This is all a bunch of garbage. The guy was crazy. It's awful, but let's not make so much of it." I want to dismiss the men at Queen's University. When the Canadian Federation of Students launched a campaign against date-rape with the slogan "No means no," they were quick to respond with their own slogans: "No means kick her in the teeth," and "No means tie me up."

Did any of you see the documentary on Colin Thatcher? One scene stays with me. He viciously slaps his "mistress" across the face and sends her sprawling. Fifteen minutes later he brings her a drink and speaks tenderly to her. She gasps, "You just slapped me in the face. Aren't you even going to say you're sorry?" Thatcher looks into her eyes and says, "I've never hit a woman in my life." There is no more room, no more time for denial. We must face the reality.

When the police officer gave the profile of Marc Lepine, he described the young man as "very gentle with women, until things didn't go his way. Then he withdrew into himself." I found this chilling. The reason is that we know that withdrawal is rage turned inward. And 85% of the men I see in counseling know only two responses to being hurt, being told "No," and being disappointed: withdrawal and rage. We punish women by withdrawal or we bully women with our size and large voices—both violent, the latter sometimes lethal.

Michelle Landsberg told a story about travelling from Edmonton to Calgary with a hockey team. They were drunk and rowdy when they boarded the plane. When the female flight attendant refused to serve any more liquor to them, they erupted with a barrage of obscenities, literally screaming at her. Landsberg surmised, and I agree, that the source of their rage was that a woman refused to service them. Deep within men, deep within our fathers and our father's fathers, is an expectation that women will be there for our every need, and when they choose to assert themselves and put themselves first, we respond by belittling women, beating up women, raping women, and even killing women.

We like to think that the next generation of boys is getting a different message, and I pray they are, but really how is this possible? Marc Lepine as a young man experienced his father beating his mother and all the children, including him. Boys are growing up in a society that still condones violence. Nintendo games entertain our boys with games that offer violence as the way to the winner's circle. The very same night that men and women huddled together against the violence in vigils, Sugar Ray Leonard and Roberto Duran were beating each other's brains out in a boxing ring, while the crowd shouted for Leonard to "Finish him off."

Ian Brown, host of *As It Happens* of CBC Radio, told a story about an experience he had the morning after the killings. He went to the bus stop to pick up his son from school. The driver of the bus was a woman. She told one of the boys to hurry up, because they were horsing around. When this boy got off the bus, he said, within earshot of Ian Brown, "If she ever tells me what to do again, I'll put a bullet through her head."

One sad thing about all this is that, predictably, it will be women who will object most vehemently to this sermon. I know this from experience. Helen Porter, member of the United Church and professional storyteller, spends a lot of time on campuses across Canada. What she hears are young women declaring themselves to be anti-feminist. They are saying that women already have equality with men, and to "harp" on equal rights is to alienate men. At one level, they ignore statistics such as 243 of the 282 seats in Parliament are held by men. At another level, they are engaged in defence of men, which is a large part of female socialization. At still another level, for many women, to take in the extent to which our society is still based on male privilege would be to take a closer look at their own relationships. Part of defending men involves protecting themselves from change, and from the subtle pervasive ways male privilege works its way into relationships. To women this morning I say: Stop defending us, stop nurturing us in unhelpful ways. It keeps us childish and irresponsible. Dorothy Dinnerstein said it best with this line, speaking to women, "If we want men to be our brothers, we have to stop treating them as if we're their mothers."

Okay, so what do we do about it? John the Baptist stands at the edge of a river, at the edge of this baptismal font, and he implores us to remember our baptisms and REPENT. It is important, especially this morning, that he is a man, one man calling other men to change and change utterly. The Pharisees and the Sadducees who are symbolic—for the writer of the gospel—of the righteous, the men beyond reproach, the churchgoers, the respected professionals, the good fathers, the community saints, approach John.

But John doesn't let them off the hook, anymore than you and I are let off the hook here this morning: "It's not enough that your father was Abraham," he tells them. There are no free rides. We're judged by our own actions, not our lineage. In fact, it's precisely because we are our father's sons that we are called to even greater change, not less.

We are, each one of us, a part of the system of patriarchy, and the call to self-scrutiny is directed at us. Not abstractly. I'm talking about going home and reflecting on the patterns in your marriage and in your home. And I challenge the women not to protect, or defend, or deny.

What else can we do? Last week, after church, the Sunday school sponsored an intergeneration lunch, and set up craft tables at which we could learn to make Christmas decorations. Doug Hall sat at one of those tables and taught me and other children how to make Christmas angels for the tree. We can give our sons memories and images of strong men making angels for Christmas trees.

We need to get together in men's groups. Not to talk about the score of last night's game, or crack jokes. We need to talk about real things together, share our fears, our struggles, support and challenge one another. Men, what happened last Wednesday night is not our fault. We are not personally responsible. But even if it's not our fault, male violence is most decidedly our problem. June Callwood suggested that men take the initiative to build shelters for violent men, so it's not the victims—women and children—who have to be uprooted for our violence.

As a society, men will have to begin taking more responsibility for the primary parenting of our children. We will need to take paternity leaves. Primary parents, usually women, are simply too powerful. This may sound like a contradiction, but it's not. Very early, it is imprinted in the brains and the nervous system that this parent literally holds the power of life and death over us. Without a lot of intentional self-reflection, that imprint remains with us into adulthood. It is branded on the eyeballs of men. So when we see a woman, when we look at our partner, we don't see a real person. We see Goddess, giver of life, nurturer of our every need, or we see Witch, who frustrates our needs, who doesn't respond fast enough to our appetites and who needs to be subdued. We see Madonna or Whore, but rarely a human person. And if you want to know whether or not women feel known and respected as persons by men, just ask your wife. Only as primary parenting is shared will women be freed to be persons with inherent dignity.

Isaiah's poem today is one of the most beautiful in the Bible. It is his vision of what the world could be like under a just and caring ruler. He presents us with images of a safe world. The lion lies down with the calf. The sheep has nothing to fear from the wolf. A child plays overtop a nest of rattlesnakes, and has nothing to fear. We need to complement his ancient vision with images of peace and safety for our world, images that seem far from reality now but which may be born into the world by God's grace. The one I'll leave you with is of a solitary woman, walking down a dimly lit street at night, vulnerable and profoundly safe. I invite you to reflect on other images that will give us hope as we journey towards the birth of a new male child.

—*December 10, 1989*

Walking Humbly Upon the Earth

MARK 10:33-36

L ast year in the "Facts and Arguments" page of *The Globe and Mail*, I read a beautiful and touching piece of writing by Alice Groeneveld. Here is an excerpt:

> Each day I see a shooting star in the vastness of our cold sky I make a wish I am shy to admit: one day to come eye to eye with a white moose. Already I can hear people snort, "A white moose! Where do you think you'll find one? Is there such a beast as a white moose?" Yes, here I can assure you. Years ago it was in the daily newspaper that two hunters had spotted a white moose somewhere in Alberta. What did they do when they got over their first surprise? They shot it. Are you silent with the news? I was.

Ms. Groeneveld continues her reflection:

> Who can shoot such a mysterious issue of nature as a white moose? I would go on my knees in awe. Well, not those hunters. They felt no inner appeal to keep those guns down. They fired. They just wanted to bag this extraordinary sample and show it off as a victory, have it mounted, sell it. An albino moose. What can better that?

This morning, I want to spend a little time talking about ecology and spirituality. Put those two terms together and one arrives at an eco-spirituality. Eco-spirituality is about our relationship with the earth, and with non-human creatures. It's about changing the fundamental way we think about our relationship with the earth and the non-human species of the earth.

That relationship underwent a dramatic change some 8,000 to 10,000 years ago. Up until that time, *Homo sapiens* understood themselves to be one species of animals among many. Like other animals, these primal peoples were nomadic. They wandered in search of food and water, taking from the earth what they needed to survive, no more, no less. Intuitively, they understood themselves to be a part of an intricate ecosystem. The earth was a living organism. Their wisdom was derived from nature itself. The earth was their sacred Mother. Like other animals, they were subject to the laws of nature. We should be grateful that we still have descendants of these primal peoples. These people were nomadic hunters and gatherers.

Then something happened. It dawned on someone that there was no need to go chasing around after animals and following the seasons and cycles of nature. You didn't need to be so dependent and vulnerable. You could domesticate the animals, plant crops, store up water and grain, and eventually build great cities. Over time, human beings discovered that, rather than be subject to the laws of nature, one could actually master nature. The agriculturalist was born. From this moment on, humanity began to separate itself from the other animals and from the earth. As in the story of the Tower of Babel, we left the earth, building towers to reach into heaven so we could be like the gods. The earth was no longer Sacred Mystery that gives and takes life, but something you could control for your own ends.

Genesis is the book of the Bible that describes this transitional era in the human beings. It is captured in the story of Cain and Abel. Abel, the firstborn, is symbolic of the hunter and gatherer. Cain, the second-born, is symbolic of the agriculturalist. And what happens in the story? Cain murders Abel. Thus begins a history of modern human's conquest over the primal peoples of the earth, the domination over the other species of the earth, and the sense that nature itself could be conquered. It is a history of violence.

It is a descendent of Cain, of course, that shot the albino moose. And shot it without any sense of sacrilege. It was a prize, a conquest, not a sentient being with any intrinsic value. We are the descendants of Cain, if truth be known. Modern humans can look at a rainforest and see only raw material to be exploited. We can gaze upon the Great Lakes, and the oceans, and see only a storage bin for our toxic wastes. We can sleep at night knowing that the blue pickerel, native exclusively to Lake Erie, is now extinct. We can capture black bears in our sights, and see at the end of the barrel $10,000 per liver. A gorilla's hand will bring $5,000 as an ashtray.

The disciples in Mark's gospel have some of Cain's blood. Jesus catches them in a prototypical Cain-like argument. After arriving at their destination, Jesus asks them: "What were you talking about on the way?" Silence fills the house. They were arguing over which one of them was the greatest. This is Cain's argument. It can be settled only with violence. It has led human beings to conquer and subdue the earth and all non-human species, to conquer and subdue other nations, other religions. It is the motivating dynamic in all domestic violence, getting straight just who exactly is in charge.

With the dawn of the enlightenment and the scientific revolution, the conquest of nature was complete. Francis Bacon could speak about putting the earth "on the rack," and torturing her until she gave us all we desired. All mystery and sacredness was lost.

The earth and all non-humans were declared devoid of spirit. It belonged to us, and there was no question about who was the greatest.

The way of Jesus is antithetical to this thinking. Greatness, Jesus offers, is about serving others, not dominating them. Jesus himself lived more like Abel than like Cain, didn't he? He was nomadic. He owned no home. "The Son of Man has nowhere to lay his head." He trusted the God of nature to provide for his daily needs. "Give us this day, our daily bread." Don't worry about what you will eat, or what to wear, said Jesus. Consider the lilies of the field. Think of the sparrow. God gives them what they need to survive. He regularly left the city and went into the wilderness to pray. In fact, Jesus drew most of his wisdom teaching and his parables from his observation of nature. And although his central concern was not for the earth per se, his spirituality was certainly grounded in a profound sense of the generosity of God, as observed through the workings of nature.

Eco-spirituality, as I said, is about changing our relationship with the earth and her species, from one of domination to one of cooperation. There is no question that already we may have done irreversible damage to the earth and therefore to our children and ourselves. It's not that we are evil. But we are living out of an old script; you might call it the story of Cain. And until we get ourselves a new story and a new spirituality, nothing is going to change. That new story, of course, is not new at all. It is 13.9 billion years old. But we may just now have the eyes to see and the ears to hear the story that the Universe and the earth are telling us. There is little use in setting targets for CO_2 emissions, in trying to determining salmon quotas, in logging companies sitting down with environmentalists to work out compromises, if we cannot agree on which story we are living out, the old one, or a new one.

Here are some principles of this ancient yet new story:

1) The earth does not belong to us. We belong to the earth.

2) The earth is God's body, the physical manifestation of Spirit. To put it poetically, "The earth is charged with the grandeur of God." It is a sacred living organism, with its own intrinsic value. What I mean by this is that the earth is more than a source of raw materials to satisfy our addiction to consumption.

3) We don't live on the earth. We are the earth in human form. The new spirituality will end a false dualism, which separates us from the earth and her creatures. We are the earth's creatures with consciousness and therefore capable of understanding that there exists no greater miracle than creation. The proper response is a religious one: awe.

4) God didn't intend evolution to end with us. We do not represent the sum total of God's imagination for the Universe. Thirteen billion years ago, God didn't think, "I am aiming for the human being, and once we've arrived there, I'm all out of ideas. That's a wrap." It's time for a serious dose of humility. God intended us to cooperate so fully with the developing Universe that we sacrifice ourselves, so that the Universe, through us, can evolve even more complex forms of life, just as the rest of the animal kingdom have given their lives for 5 billion years so that we could assume this form.

5) In the new eco-spirituality, we have to go beyond the

metaphor of stewardship as that term is commonly understood. As it's understood in Genesis, being a steward means that God has entrusted the earth to us, and we are to take care of it. But, the bio-spiritual truth is that we belong to the earth. The idea of taking care of the earth is a kind of benevolent arrogance, once we realize that the earth takes care of us. In the 21st century, what we are being called to do is not so much to take of the earth, as to take our place in the ecosystem, as one species among many. This should evoke in us a renewed gratitude, and a renewed humility.

This morning, I offer no practical solution to our environmental crisis. I offer a sensibility from which to begin discussions among business, environmentalists and governments of the world: We are the earth, and so our destiny is the destiny of the earth. This is the spiritual issue of the 21st century. The church needs to be a leader in eco-spirituality. It is, as Father Thomas Berry has stated, "The Great Commissioning" of our lives.

I'll end with a quote from Meister Eckhart, a 14th-century Christian mystic and theologian:

Apprehend God in all things,
for God is in all things.
Every single creature is full of God
and is a book about God.
Every creature is a word of God.
If I spent enough time with the tiniest creature,
even a caterpillar,
I would never have to prepare a sermon.
So full of God is every creature.

—*October 19, 1997*

Get Thee to Nineveh!

When God saw how they turned from their evil ways, God changed his mind and saved the Ninevites. But this was very displeasing to Jonah.

Talk about a reluctant prophet! God says, "Go to the Ninevites, and tell them to repent!" Jonah says, "Sorry, I'm the wrong man for the job. As a faithful Jew I hate the Ninevites; always have, always will!" Then he hops on the first ship out of Israel to try to get away from God. But a big storm comes up and the sailors want to know why God is punishing them. They figure out that it must be the landlubber who is turning green on deck. Jonah says, "Yeah, I'm the trouble here. Chuck me overboard, and your problems will cease. So they do, and sure enough the seas quiet. When he gets swallowed by a whale, and spends three days and three nights in its belly, he realizes there's something fishy going down. The big fish vomits him up on shore, and once again God says to him, "Jonah, go to the Ninevites and tell them to repent!" So Jonah drags his prophetic heels to Nineveh, issues his warning, and his worst nightmare comes true. He's successful! They repent. This infuriates him. He says to God, "I knew something like this would happen. I can't believe you'd forgive the Ninevites. Then he throws a tantrum, asking a second time to be killed. Three times Jonah welcomes the death sentence. The story ends with Jonah sulking under a withered desert bush.

What are we to make of this? And what on earth does this story have to do with today? First of all, let's give Jonah a break. The Ninevites were, after all, the enemy. He was taught in his religion to despise Ninevites, perhaps even to pray that God would destroy Nineveh. Now he's hearing that God loves even Ninevites and wants to give them a second chance. He's thinking to himself: "It can't be true, it can't be true."

But there are two kinds of truth. There's the homespun version of truth. It goes down as easy as mother's milk. God hates Ninevites. And then there is a more foreign truth. God's love extends even to the enemy. This goes down like bad medicine. It might be good for us, but that doesn't make it any easier to take. Jonah would rather die than believe this deeper truth. The journey from the homespun truth to the deep, strange truth that's hard to swallow is the journey to Nineveh. And if you think the road is smooth, think again. The deeper truth shattered Jonah.

Each of us has had to make this journey to Nineveh, kicking and screaming and dragging our heels, at one point or another. I know I have. When I was growing up, I knew in my bones that gay people were freaks. Once, in a display of machismo, I agreed they should all be lined up and shot. Of course, I didn't know any gay men. In my white suburban culture, it didn't matter. They were the enemy of Marlborough Man. That's all I needed to know. Then I met a man who became my friend. After we were friends, he told me he was gay. I was stopped in my macho tracks, turned around, inside out. I was on my way to Nineveh! I was in a whale's belly, on a voyage not of my own choosing. My homespun, middle-class suburban truth was shattered by the deeper truth embodied in my new friend.

Let me give you another example of how one limited truth can get swallowed up by a deeper truth, leaving us groping in the dark. When people come into counseling, they hold cherished truths about family. "My father was the greatest man, kind, always there for us. My mother was absolutely the best mother I could have hoped for. I had a perfectly normal family when I was growing up." Invariably, as details of the story emerge, people hear themselves saying things that paint a little different picture. "Well, he drank a bit too much at times, and every now and then he threw us around a bit, but he loved us, he did. I never could understand why Mom didn't try to stop him." The story darkens as the truth deepens.

It's not easy to face the truth. We want to run like Jonah in the opposite direction. But, if we're lucky, the truth pursues us like a Hound From Heaven, and won't let us go. We end up in the belly of a whale, being carried kicking and screaming toward that "great city," Nineveh, the city of Truth. Now I enjoy a more authentic relationship with my family. I can see them for who they are, and love them more because of it.

But when we're going through the transformation, it feels like death. And it is, in a way. As in a dream, something has to be sacrificed. Either we sacrifice the old self to make room for the new, or we sacrifice the Truth. Jonah's way out of this dilemma is to want to kill himself, but that's a cop-out. Fundamentalism's way out is to sacrifice God's truth, settling instead for rigid dogma. But the faithful road is the road to Nineveh, risking our own transformation over and over again.

I remember my first year of seminary. I went in with a rock solid faith. The Bible was the literal word of God, each word dictated by the Holy Spirit to a scribe. I had the truth, "praise God!" Then the word of the Lord came to me in a delightful New Testament professor, Dr. Heinz Guenther. One day, he took me aside, and said, "Bruce, God gave you a wonderful mind. Think! Think!" In one year, my rock solid ground of my faith, based upon a literal understanding of the Bible, turned to mush! An earthquake struck. I was frightened, disoriented. I was in the belly of a whale, not knowing where I would end up. But, you know what? When I finally got spit up on shore again, I was a new person. The Bible came alive for me in a new and life-affirming way. I could not have arrived there without traveling that long dark year.

In the church, we really should have more festivals of darkness. We have only one day in the whole year when the lights go out and the sanctuary becomes a whale's belly. That's Good Friday, and no one comes to church because it's such a "downer." But without darkness there is no transformation; without fish bellies, and caves, without hellish confusion, church becomes superficial and over time, irrelevant. k.d. lang, in her song, *Outside Myself*, has a line that expresses this:

I have been in a storm of the sun
Basking, senseless to what I've become
I was a fool to worship just light,
When after all, it follows night.

You've probably read in the papers this past week about an 82-year-old lawyer, Clarence Walsh, who has just completed an intensive seven-year report on the Iran-Contra Affair. He establishes once and for all that the official state presentation of the truth was in fact a lie. There is no question, for example, that George Bush was fully aware of what was happening, even though he went on national TV to deny it. I remember when I first read

Noam Chomsky, a professor of linguistics at MIT, banned for 20 years by the American media. In a book called *Manufacturing Consent*, he painstakingly documents how the American government has fine-tuned the art of manufacturing consent in the public to the most inhumane policies and practices. Vietnam was considered a failure by the White House, not because it was a poor decision that killed thousands of young men but rather because it was the only time in the last 50 years when they failed to manufacture consent. The root of the problem was that they didn't control the media. Desert Storm was the correction. It was a masterpiece in public relations.

Some part of me doesn't want to know this. It is dark. I want to believe that the official truth is God's truth. I want it straight and simple. God hates Ninevites, gays are sick, my family is perfect, the Bible is the literal Word of God, and the state always tells the truth. Being swallowed up by deeper truths is messy and disorienting. But alas, it is the Biblical way. God's truth is always deeper, more complex and ambiguous than our own. And the moment we want to close it off, package it and put it in our back pocket, we get the call to go to Nineveh.

At the end of the story, Jonah is bitterly angry with God for destroying a bush that was protecting him from the bright sun. Again, Jonah wants to die. But what he is really angry about is that God won't shelter him from the truth. God asks Jonah: "Are you concerned about the death of a single bush? Yet you would let 120,000 perish?" God persists right up until the end with Jonah, trying to talk some sense into his head and some love into his heart. The good news is that God won't shelter us from the truth, but God will go with us to Nineveh. I'll end with a poem you might be familiar with:

And I said to the man who stood at the gate of the year: give me a light that I may tread safely into the unknown; and he replied, "Go out into the darkness and put your hand into the hand of God; that shall be to you better than light, and safer than a known way."

—January 23, 1994

Who Is My Family?

"Who are my mother and my brothers?" And looking around
at the crowd he said, "Here are my mother and my brothers."

ho is my family? That's the question Jesus asks when he hears that his mother and siblings are outside asking for him. A friend of mine goes into congestive heart failure. She calls her brother and sister in the United States. They either don't believe her or don't seem particularly interested, and certainly neither one is able to come at this time. She has to turn to her friends for help. She asks herself, "Who is my family?" A gay man decides to come out to his parents and his siblings; they reject him. He asks, "Who is my family?" A young black woman, in the film *Secrets and Lies*, decides to search out her biological mother after the death of her adoptive parents. Her mother turns out to be white. She asks, "Who is my family?" A middle-aged woman goes into therapy because she can't stand her husband's touch. She faces what she has always known she would have to face: her father and his friends sexually abused her repeatedly as a child. She confronts her father, and her mother, sisters and brothers ostracize her for doing so. She asks, "Who is my family?"

This morning, I want to talk about family from a Christian perspective. Everyone agrees on the importance of family. Most agree that we need to return to some solid family values. Certainly our federal politicians know this. All of them, with the exception, I

203

believe, of Alexa McDonough, appeared for their post-election speeches with their family by their side. Great optics. All of them presenting themselves as the ideal nuclear family. American politicians all publicly confess their belief in the family as the foundational institution of civilization. Not to do so would be political suicide. The driving force behind religiously right organizations like the Promise Keepers, a Christian men's movement, is a return to Biblically based family values.

We naturally assume we can turn to our spiritual leaders for unambiguous support. Jesus and family values go hand in hand, don't they? Well, what are we to make from what we heard a few minutes ago from Mark's gospel? Jesus finishes a healing spree and the crowd follows him home, wanting more of the same. His family is clearly concerned about him. He's accused of being the son of Satan, deriving his healing power from an evil source. Jesus answers with characteristically colourful logic. Why would Satan, who causes sickness, according to first-century Jewish beliefs, want to heal these people? "No," says Jesus, "my healing is a sign that I am Satan's nemesis, not his servant."

All this talk is worrying his family. They come out to "restrain him"; in other words, to shut him up. Jesus gets a message that his mother and brothers and sisters want a word with him. Simple request.

Jesus' response to that simple request should give us pause. "Who are my mother and my brothers and sisters?" He distances himself from them. Imagine how his mother must have felt at that moment. What about his brothers and sisters? If they ever needed confirmation that Jesus was indeed losing his mind, this was it. In first-century Judaism, family was everything. What's going on? In fact, we know Jesus' attitude about family through only three passages in the whole Second Testament. Besides this reference there is the occasion when someone says to him, "Blessed is the womb that bore you, and the breasts that suckled you." Again, Jesus is not exactly gushing with a son's love for his mother. "How fortunate, rather, are those who listen to God's teaching and observe it." Then in Luke's gospel, Jesus tells a crowd that he has come to brandishing a sword, his purpose to divide the family up, not bring peace to it. You didn't hear that from any of the politicians in the federal elections.

Here is the sobering reality of the gospels. When Jesus does talk about the family, he is almost savage in his attack on it, as it was known in the Mediterranean world. It won't do to simplistically invoke the name of Jesus in support of a return to family values. As usual, Jesus of Nazareth undermines conventional sentiment and morality for the sake of a deeper unconventional ethic that goes by the name of the Kingdom of God.

The family in first-century Mediterranean culture was a reflection of society in miniature, as it is today. In the family, we learn patterns of love, hate, helping, abusing, etc. It's also where we learn about power, and that power is reflected in the relationships between family members.

Here's what we know about how family was organized 2,000 years ago in Mediterranean society. First of all, it was hierarchical and patriarchal. Men were the head of the household; women were subservient. Men could divorce women with a piece of paper. Women had so such privilege. Women were legally the property of men. Children had no rights whatsoever. They, too, were the property of men, and could be disposed of at will. Boys were more treasured than girls, and there are many recorded instances of female infanticide in the Roman era. The family, in other words, was the institution that both reflected and perpetuated an ethic of male privilege and domination.

205

The Bible, with the notable exception of Jesus of Nazareth, supports this social arrangement. Only 20 years after the death of Jesus, St. Paul softens Jesus' radical message. Rather than undermine the hierarchical and patriarchal nature of the family, he attempts to humanize it. This is what right-wing religious movements like the Promise Keepers do as well. Basically, they accept that this system of domination was instituted by God, because it's in the Bible. Men are the head of the household, but they should be servant leaders. Women are to be subservient, but respected. But this much is clear. Jesus himself wasn't interested in merely humanizing the social arrangement. He intended to subvert it.

Well, that was 2,000 years ago. Family is different now, right? Well, in many ways, it is, of course. But even in our 20th-century democratic society, there are painful vestiges of that system of domination and submission, and male privilege. Let me offer two.

The first has to do with how couples divide up the household chores. Ann and I have been doing pre-marriage courses for the last six years. We began with the assumption that these young men and women who came to our course were committed to equality. This would be reflected in the fair division of household tasks. Wrong. Although these couples were both working eight to ten hours a day, what we discovered was that after work, women were still doing 80% of the housework, and men 20%. On average, we have found that it takes between 18 and 25 hours per week to do the household chores. If our courses reflect society as a whole, and there is solid research to support this, then women are spending a full two to three working days outside their jobs, while men spend about half a day on these chores. Although we may smile in recognition, and regard this as sort of cute, this reflects an area of assumed male privilege. Spread out over a lifetime, there are very real quality-of-life issues at stake. Jesus came to break up such patterns of inequity and male privilege.

The second vestige of this system of domination and submission which Jesus sought to subvert is a more tragic one: family violence. Although there are instances of such violence originating with women, the overwhelming evidence is that family violence is a male phenomenon. And when you spend much time talking to men who sexually or physically abuse their wives and children, you realize that at the core of this behaviour is a single deep-seated attitude. That attitude is one of ownership. An abuser believes that his wife and children are his property, and he can do with them whatever he pleases. They belong to him. Where does that come from? It is a vestige of the politics of domination, and sadly this politic rears its ugly head in every century.

It is precisely these attitudes that Jesus could not abide. Family life, like all human life, comes under the critique of the Kingdom of God, including Jesus' own family. It doesn't matter to Jesus how good you look on the outside to the rest of the community; impressions on national TV might count in the polling stations but not in the Kingdom.

The flip side of this is that in the Kingdom of God, there are all kinds of family configurations that fall outside conventional notions of family, that don't fit the mould, but which are unquestionably good families: single-parent families, gay and lesbian families, families with stepparents. What matters is not the form, but the substance, the quality of relationships among members. If they are based on mutual respect, a willingness to listen deeply, and a conscious decision to extend oneself for the well-being of the other, that is family. If our children are taught to value diversity, to love God, to respect themselves and others; and that people of different colour, gender, sexual orientation, and religion are equal before God, that is the kind of family Jesus of Nazareth would call his own.

There is a scene in the movie *Sling Blade*, in which the mildly retarded Carl gets out of prison and returns home to visit his father. His purpose is to kill him, for all the abuse he suffered by his father's hand. But after seeing him, a pathetic old man talking to himself in a chair all alone, Carl changes his mind and walks away. In the next scene, Joe-Bob is baptized in the river. He had no choice about his biological family. But he is able to choose his spiritual family. Some of us were born into wonderful families— kind, caring, and nurturing. Others, like Carl, were less fortunate. For good or bad, we had no choice. But there is another family we can belong to only by choice. We can choose to belong to the family of Jesus Christ. We can choose to learn the will of God and do it. When we do, Jesus calls us his own.

—June 8, 1997

Light It Up

EXODUS 24:12-18; MATTHEW 17:1-9

Jesus was transfigured before them and his face shone like the sun and his clothes became dazzling white.

John left his office tower every night at the same time and boarded the train to go home to his wife and daughter. He did wills and estates for a large law firm downtown. This had been his life for the last 20 years, and it was a pretty good life, by all accounts. But one night on his way home, he saw something that would change his life. He looked out of the window of the train on his way home and saw a neon sign, Mitzie's Ballroom, in bright pink letters. Something stirred in him. Night after night as the train passed by, that sign beckoned. Then, one night, he found himself getting off the train, following the sign, and walking up the long flight of stairs to Mitzie's. He began to find excuses for coming home late on Wednesday nights and became a secret ballroom dancer. Some unlived life in him began to stir. There was no denying it and no turning back. John was going to dance. So begins the story of recent re-release of the film *Shall We Dance?*

What happened on that mountaintop, for Peter and James and John? I suspect that whatever it was, it was on a continuum with what happened back down at sea level the first time they met Jesus. By the shores of Galilee, this man lit up like a sign, stirring in them a promise of new life. If you believe the story, they simply left everything they had known and identified with and followed him. The mountaintop experience was a 1,000-watt version of that first experience. Jesus lit up, and more importantly, he lit them up. There was no denying it and there was no turning back. They intended to follow this light. Can that happen? Can this kind of extraordinary thing happen to ordinary people? I think it can and it does.

The first time I encountered Jesus was at an evangelical rally. The preacher told me that he was "the way, the truth and the life," and for whatever reason, I believed him. He shone for me as a beacon of light. I left everything and followed. I left my identity as a jock, which pretty much defined me at the time. I left my family and friends. I didn't stop loving them, of course. But I wanted to follow Jesus and, for me, that meant studying theology, which meant going to Toronto. Basically, I just left behind my old self, like an old coat that had served me well, and followed.

What happened? Jesus became a shining icon for me. God shone through him, and it connected with something so deep inside of me that I'm almost tempted to say I had no choice. Of course, I did have a choice. We always do. But this shining light drew out of me a desire that was more ancient and primal than hunger or thirst. That happens. It happens at sea level, in the midst of our daily routine, taking care of business, on the way home from work, and it happens intensively in mountaintop experiences. Now for me there was a lot of baggage that came along with my experience of Jesus; people were telling me things I had to believe to be saved, and it took a couple of years to deprogram from the dogma piled high on top of the experience itself. But the bottom line was there was no going back.

God shone through Jesus at that rally and I lit up with a love I hadn't known. We come into the world fired with love and joy and predisposed to fall head over heels in love with the world. All we need is someone to witness our uniqueness, a few good people to attune to our desires who will be a good enough mirror to reflect our wonderfulness to us. When this happens, we shine with holy light. We know that we're from God and that we carry with us into this world a unique gift that we are meant to give to the world. When we are expressing that gift, when we are not afraid of loving or being loved, we are filled with joy.

We know this. It is why we are drawn to newborns and infants before, as Bruce Cockburn puts it, "the strangeness" sets in. "The strangeness" is life without love and joy. The closed heart is an unnatural state of being. The church calls it sin, and freighted as the word is, we haven't really found a better one to describe the experience. Sin is the state of alienation from God, others, the earth, and ourselves. It seeps into our lives from many sources—from emotional and psychological trauma, from dysfunctional social and political systems—and it manifests in attitudes and behaviours contrary to our nature.

Sin closes the heart and snuffs out the light. Our Christian story tells us that, in and through Jesus and his teachings, hardened hearts begin to soften. He gets through to the not-quite-doused light in our heart. At first all we are aware of is a deep yearning. We sense that we're not fully manifesting the love and the joy that is in every cell of our bodies. We have a cellular memory of a time before the strangeness. To dwell in the presence of Christ is to have this yearning triggered for "Something More." We tend to confuse this Something More with stuff like money and houses and cars, and we can get addicted to these things. But what we're looking for is a way back to the unprotected heart, a way back to the Love and to the Joy that is a symptom of having been apprehended by it.

Christ isn't the only light, of course, and the light doesn't just shine through church windows. God is far more generous than that. For those with eyes to see and who are listening deeply, God is everywhere and in every faith beckoning; sometimes God speaks from neon signs. But Jesus is our light and it is a distinctive light. It's easy for us to get caught up in thinking that what we're about as a church is running the church, isn't it? We've got to meet the budget, put a roof on the sanctuary, deliver the next program, keep things running, and of course, we do. But this is not what we are ultimately about when it gets right down to it, is it? If Christ doesn't shine through our activities, we might just as well stop what we are doing. If Christ doesn't light up this sanctuary on a Sunday morning, we might just as well mute the organ, not to mention the preacher, and go home. If Christ is not shining through us, through you and me and all that we do, then we may be missing the point.

In his novel, *Empire Falls*, Richard Russo speculates that Jesus' disciples must have experienced some ambivalence after his death. He writes, "They never wanted him crucified of course, but what a relief it must have been when the stone was rolled across the entrance of the tomb, sealing everything shut so they could go back to being fishermen which they knew how to do." I wonder if what frightened Peter on that mountaintop was more than just the dazzling light transfiguring Jesus? I wonder if he intuited that the reason Jesus took the three of them up there in the first place was that the time was coming, very soon, when the light would have to shine through them? Maybe it wasn't Jesus' transfiguration but a premonition of his own transfiguration which scared Peter. So he built three booths, one each for Moses, Elijah, and Jesus, because this would keep the deal out there, between God and the special people. He knew how to handle special people. You make monuments to them. What he didn't know how to do was to let this same light shine through him.

Well, the good news is that Christ is alive and still shines through the likes of you and me and Peter. That can be kind of heavy, I know, to think of ourselves as the transfigured presence of Christ. But this might help: Ann still has her mother's china, which was passed to her mother by her mother's mother. Much of it is chipped and cracked and it's all very fragile, but it is still fine china. And when you hold it up to the light, you can see right through it. It's not that we're such good, moral, solid citizens that the light of Christ shines through us, but that we're made so fine and so fragile by God. We can "forget our perfect offerings," in the words of Leonard Cohen. "There is a crack in everything. That's how the light gets in." It's our transparency and vulnerability, not our strength and power, that God needs for the light to shine through.

You see, it was the voice of fear that sounded in Peter at first. But another voice sounded on that mountaintop: "This is my Beloved, listen to Him." I take this to mean that we have a choice about which voice we are going to listen to: the voice of fear or the Voice which calls us to fall back in love with the world, with the earth, with our partners, with Love itself. This is a voice inviting us to bask in the light of Christ so that we may ourselves become the cracked and fragile vessels through which the light of Christ can shine.

February 6, 2005

The Weight of These Sad Times

MARK 6:30-44

But Jesus answered them, "you give them something to eat."

We celebrated New Year's Eve by having some friends over for dinner. We enjoyed ourselves immensely over good food, good conversation, and a modest amount of wine. We shared highlights from the past year and then spoke aloud our intentions for 2005. But when midnight struck, we decided against breaking open another bottle of bubbly. I awoke thinking about the evening, and the word that best described it for me was *subdued*. I can't speak for the others, but I realized that, for me, our celebration was tinged with a quiet, unspoken grief. How could it have been otherwise, in light of the tsunami tragedy in Southeast Asia? One of Shakespeare's memorable lines came to me, from the final scenes of King Lear, as the stage is strewn with dead bodies: Edgar concludes the play with the observation, "the weight of these sad times we must obey; speak what we feel and not what we ought to say." I suspect that our New Year's celebration obeyed the weight of these sad times.

One of the worst natural disasters in human history is unfolding on the other side of the planet in Indonesia, Thailand, Sri Lanka, and India. The death toll is over 150,000 and most are expecting it to go much higher. It is very difficult to allow the weight of human suffering to bear down on us. I've heard it said that, excluding the two world wars, this is the first natural disaster to affect the entire world. Over 40 nationalities were represented among those who lost their lives. Psychologists tell us that a psychic numbing anaesthetizes us in the face of this kind of disaster. Michael Enright on CBC said that it requires an act of will to overcome this numbing.

You may have seen the front page of *The Globe and Mail* yesterday. A tourist couple sit in their bathing suits on a beach in Phuket, Thailand, under an umbrella. One is sunbathing. The other is looking at a scene of devastation behind him left by the tsunami. The caption reads, "Tourists soak up rays at a resort in Thailand, disconnected from the chaos from last week's tsunami." At first I felt a surge of judgment. How could anyone be so insensitive as to be vacationing in the midst of such suffering? But then I realized we have no way of knowing what is in their hearts. They may have decided to keep their vacation, knowing that the country was dependent on tourism. They may have spent the morning helping with the clean-up and decided to take a break on the beach. But taken by itself, the absurdity of the image speaks to how difficult it is for us to be connected to such overwhelming tragedy. It is a stark image of denial and, as such, it belongs on a continuum of denial strategies.

Rex Murphy wrote a very moving column about a different, yet no less grotesque manifestation of denial by developed nations. He was asking what it means that Reality TV shows like *Survivor* can capture the attention of millions of wealthy North Americans and Europeans. The whole sordid spectacle is a mock-up of actual disasters, like the one happening in reality. We are asked to believe that this made-for-TV mock-up has something to do with surviving a disaster. The winner gets a million bucks; the losers merely go home, family still intact, roofs over their heads, jobs waiting. The fact that we play "pretend survival" when two-thirds of the world is struggling day in and day out to survive displays a shocking capacity for denial. We can only hope that shows like *Survivor* will themselves be swept away by this most recent disaster.

For many, "the weight of these sad times" will demand an answer to the question: "Where is God in all of this?" Defending God in times like this is certainly not at the top of the emergency response list of things needing attention. However, I also know that for many people, Christians included, natural disasters are at the top of the list of reasons why belief is difficult at best and impossible for some. I will simply say a few words about this and then move on.

The average person of faith believes in a God who is all-powerful and in absolute control of the Universe. This is the characteristic that makes God "God" for most of us. What good is a God who is not in control of everything? There are real problems with this belief. Besides the problem of free will that this belief undermines, it raises critical problems in the face of natural disasters. Why would God let this happen? You read stories of people who have lost their entire family, wandering around looking beneath the rubble for any sign of their loved ones, fathers carrying their dead babies in their arms, whole rooms full of infants who were washed up on shore, waiting for identification.

The traditional theological response to such innocent suffering is that there are things we just don't understand. God's ways are not our ways. But, we are assured, God has a plan and even natural disasters and the suffering they cause are part of that plan. The corollary to this way of thinking, sometimes stated openly and sometimes merely implied, is that this was God's will. As a minister, I would never be able to find the courage, or whatever it takes, to tell this to that father holding his drowned infant in his arms. More importantly I don't think it's true.

I have come to the conclusion that we have placed far too much stock in omnipotence as a defining characteristic of God. If God had the power to stop this earthquake, or prevent the Holocaust, or the Rwandan genocide, but chose not to for whatever reasons, it leaves me with a God I cannot believe in. Process theology believes that it is the nature of God to place limits on God's own power, limits which cannot be suspended. God empties God's self of absolute power in order to make room for actual freedom in creation.

In so doing, God confers upon all of creation, including human beings, the dignity of freedom; in creation, this freedom manifests as the capacity for self-organization. Sometimes this means a seismic shift below the earth's surface, which can have terrible consequences for us. In human beings, the dignity of freedom implies the possibility that this freedom will be used in the service of evil.

The defining characteristic of God is not in the capacity to control the Universe but in the abiding Biblical promise to be present to us and with us in all circumstances as the non-coercive presence of Love and Compassion. Where is God in this disaster? God is in the weeping of the father for his child. God is in the inconsolable grief of the woman who has lost everything and everyone. God weeps with us and through us. It is a central feature of our Christian story that God did not intervene to stop the execution of his faithful child on the cross. Rather, we claim, God entered into his suffering on the cross. In identifying with his suffering, God also identifies with the suffering of humanity. God is a suffering Presence with those who suffer.

But God is present as well in the human inclination to respond with love and compassion to tragedy. In our Christian story, this is the story of Easter. Love and compassion cannot be executed, nor can they be swept away by natural disaster. They will rise up again.

There is another tsunami rushing towards the devastation in South and Southeast Asia. It is a tsunami of compassion, a tide that more than rivals the tides of destruction. On CBC, I heard story after story of how ordinary Canadians, private citizens, and small businesses have raised over $20 million. I am certain that larger corporations are already mobilizing their ranks to contribute to relief effort. Worldwide, it is estimated that billions of dollars of donations have been sent to help with the relief work. God is also present as compassionate response, ensuring that senseless death will not have the last word.

Imagine if we were able to harness this tide of compassion, not just in response to disasters but in response to the ongoing economic injustice that renders this part of the world poor and our part of the world rich. Long after this wave of destruction has passed, after villages have been rebuilt, as they shall be rebuilt, long after these resilient people find a way to go on living even in the midst of their grief, life will return to normal for them. "The trouble with normal," as Bruce Cockburn wrote, "is it always gets worse." Unless we do something.

The median charitable donation for Canadians is around $200 per year. This means that an equal number of people give above and below this amount. What is rarely mentioned is that only 25% of Canadians make a claim for a charitable donation. It is a sign of great hope, therefore, that Statistics Canada will show a surge of charitable giving in the year 2004. But what about 2005, 2006, and 2007, when the seas are quiet and sand is warm underfoot on the resort beaches of Thailand? It is a question of some import whether we will collectively return to our beach chairs in a few months.

When the disciples saw the enormity of the need before them, they questioned Jesus about whether or not there were the resources to feed all of them. Likewise, millions await our help. At first, the best suggestion the disciples could come up with was to instruct Jesus to tell them to go home and fend for themselves. Jesus' response is characteristically blunt: "You give them something to eat." The need is enormous, overwhelming in fact. Our Lord has confidence in our capacity to multiply what we've been given in the service of those who have so little. The miracle of the multiplication of loaves and fishes happened before the disciples' eyes and it is happening before our own eyes. May our compassion as a nation, as a community of faith, and as individuals multiply and be distributed among the hungry and thirsty, the grieving, and the homeless.

—January 2, 2005

Born From Above
(Again and Again)

GENESIS 12:1-4; JOHN 3:1-17

The wind blows where it chooses and you hear the sound of it,
but you don't know where it comes from or where it goes.

There's a difference between being "born again" and "born from above." Once a week, I have a telephone conversation with a woman who used to be a client of mine. When I came out to BC, she still needed a little support so we have our talks. She's a born-again Christian who doesn't have much patience for my Christianity, because she tells me I'm not born-again. Neither are most of the people in the United Church of Canada for that matter, as far as she is concerned. We don't "believe" the Bible or that Jesus died for our sins. And that's not good.

A radio host interviewed a seven-year-old about her faith. "How long have you been a born-again Christian?" he asked her. The little girl told him that she had been a Christian since she was three. And what happens to people who don't believe in Jesus? "They go straight to hell," she responded.

Jesus tells Nicodemus he must be "born from above." Nicodemus is the one who gets a little confused at this point and asks Jesus how it's possible to re-enter his mother's womb and be "born again." It's ironic that this misunderstanding has spawned a whole branch of the church that calls itself "born-again Christians."

Now, I have met many wonderful people who refer to themselves as born-again Christians and I've met a few who are more frightening. My point is not to denigrate brothers and sisters in the faith but rather to explore the rich possibilities of what might be meant by being "born from above," as distinct from being "born-again."

In a recent episode of ER, the head nurse, Kerri, gets a telephone message from her birth mother, whom she's never met. Kerri decides to meet her mother for dinner. Kerri pulls out a photo of her son. Kerri's deceased life partner, a woman, with whom she parented their son, is also in the photo. Her mother assumes she's a nanny. Kerri tells her she's gay. But her mother is a born-again Christian. She offers to pray for Kerri's healing so that she might get over it. Kerri just wants to be accepted for who she is. Her mother's born-again faith cannot go there. Kerri is forced to walk away from her mother.

Jesus tells Nicodemus that in order to see the Kingdom of God one must be born from above. The born-again position of Kerri's mother prevented her from seeing the Kingdom of God revealed in her long-lost daughter. She missed a great opportunity to be born from above. To be born from above means to be radically open to what the Wind blows your way, to the Stranger whom you wouldn't choose to have in your life, to the threatening idea, to the Holy Other which may just subvert your dogmas and even your carefully constructed identity. It means that, if there's a choice between your beliefs and your daughter, you choose your daughter every time.

Jesus tells Nicodemus: "The Spirit blows where it will." In Hebrew and Greek, wind and spirit are translated from the same word. You don't know where the wind comes from or where it's going, but you can hear it as it passes. It's beyond our control. All we can do is be open to the possibility that sacred seeds are carried by that wind. The Spirit blows into our carefully constructed lives and, if we have a feel for the wind, we'll have to expand our hearts and our minds to make room for the life it lays at our doorstep.

Ann and I are approaching our 18th wedding anniversary. Some of you will have noticed there is a significant age difference between us. Now 20 years ago or so, when we fell in love, we couldn't possibly have imagined all the implications surrounding this age difference. For example, we never had a conversation about the fact that I just might end up being a grandfather at the tender age of 44.

A few weeks ago, we received confirmation that Henry was bringing his little sister, Nora, and his parents to Vancouver for a two-week visit, during which time grandma and grandpa will be going solo for four days with the grandchildren. Now, you might think that this news was the source of unrestrained joy inside of me, but you're wrong. How was I supposed to get my work done? Where would I be sleeping? How would I have any free time to work out, or to go to the driving range, or drink a cup of tea in peace? Assuming the identity and role of grandfather was a force that blew into my life over which I had no control. But as I open to it, I might just be born from above. There are transcendent possibilities here for me, possibilities that come from above and beyond what my ego thinks I want.

Susan, our Minister of Pastoral Care, finds herself developing relationships with those who live on the streets around her apartment. She does not know why she is suddenly noticing these men who are mostly invisible to society. A wind blew across her heart and opened her eyes. Susan will tell you that she comes from a privileged background. These strange and mysterious "others" have crossed her path and opened her up to a whole new way of seeing things. She's being born from above.

The witness of Scripture is clear that, as often as not, this is the way God works. God comes to us sometimes as an Other, from somewhere beyond our choosing and our control, in five-year-olds and two-year-olds, in homeless men, in a lesbian daughter, in a peasant rabbi whose name is Jesus. And if we dare to open to these gifts of the wind, we will have to expand our hearts and our minds because the hearts and the minds we have right now are simply too small to accommodate the life we're being offered by the Spirit.

Nicodemus comes to Jesus under cover of night. As a respected religious scholar, to be seen approaching this peasant rabbi with anything but some free advice would be regarded as shameful. But somehow he intuits that his heart and his mind, his role, his beliefs, his way of being are simply too small for the promptings of the Spirit. Rather than put down Nicodemus as a blind Pharisee, as too many sermons have done, let's focus on his openness. He shows up, whereas most of his colleagues shut down. What many of you may not know is that Nicodemus shows up once again at the end of the story, this time in the clear light of day, with extravagant amounts of oils and spices to anoint the lifeless body of the man who changed his life. He opens his heart, even when what the Spirit blew his way was death.

This discipline of opening our heart to what the Spirit blows our way, in life and in death, is the key to receiving what Jesus of John's gospels calls "eternal life." Jesus didn't hold eternal life up as a reward for those who believe the right things about him, or threaten those who don't with eternal damnation. One shudders at how that little girl's heart and mind were closed down at such an early age. I think Jesus was telling us we can be born from above, again and again and again, eternally. Such is God's love for the world, and for you, that you may know the gift of eternal life here and now. As we receive the bread and wine this morning, let us open our hearts to what the Wind is blowing our way.

—February 20, 2005

The Quiet Centre

GENESIS 2:15-17; 3:1-7: MATTHEW 4:1-11

*"Did God say you shall not eat from the fruit
of any tree in the garden?"*

Come and find the quiet centre, in the crowded life we lead
find the room for hope to enter, find the frame where we are
    freed:
clear the chaos and the clutter, clear our eyes that we may see
all the things that really matter, be at peace and simply be.

Ahhh ... Everybody now all together—breathe. What a concept! Finding a quiet centre in this crowded life we lead. Finding a frame where we are freed. Now, I realize that these words would mean something different to everyone in this sanctuary this morning. But I think we could get general agreement that finding a quiet centre would be a good thing.

How strange it is that we seem to choose the path of disquiet rather than of peace. Ann reminded me of a French film made in 1965, called *Le Bonheur* (Happiness). It tells the story of a man who has a nearly perfect life. He is happily married. He has two wonderful children. Every Sunday, the family goes to the park for a picnic. Then one day at the post office, he begins to flirt with the teller. He falls in love with her as well, and decides he wants to have both women. He's sure his wife will understand. He uses the metaphor of an apple orchard to help her understand. Outside their lovely orchard, in the next field over, there is another tree, filled with blossoms and wonderful fruit. More fruit, more happiness. Surely she understands. Later that afternoon, his wife drowns herself.

I wonder what God meant when God told the primal couple in the garden that, if they ate the fruit of the tree in the centre of the garden, they would surely die. Adam and Eve have an idyllic life. All their needs are met. They have a lovely garden to grow. As well, they are totally free to enjoy the fruit of any tree in the garden, except for the fruit of the Tree of the Knowledge of Good and Evil. Enter the serpent, agent of anxiety, and planter of disturbing questions. "Did God say you couldn't eat of the fruit of any tree in the garden?" Eve tells the serpent no, it was just the one tree she couldn't eat the fruit from. But the serpent has already done the deed. He has shifted her attention away from the abundance she enjoys and onto the one thing she cannot have and before long wants. Desire for more is awakened in her.

The serpent convinces her that God is just blowing smoke. She won't die if she eats the fruit, like God says. Her eyes will be opened and she'll know the difference between good and evil. God, whispers the serpent, just doesn't want any rivals in this department. The serpent is a liar, of course. All God said was not to eat the fruit of the Tree of the Knowledge of Good and Evil. It's the serpent that introduces the idea that she'll gain the capacity to judge accurately between good and evil. But what if just the opposite happens when we reach for the low-hanging fruit of the desire for more? What if our capacity to judge between good and evil becomes skewed by it?

What if our moral and ethical judgment is fatally compromised because now we serve a god whose name is Just a Little More?

What God knows is that when the desire for more blinds us to the abundance we already have, it becomes, functionally, our god. And God knows that this god will destroy us and everything in its path, starting with our capacity to discern good and evil. I know, we've been taught to associate the Fall with sexual indiscretion. The reason is that, in the story, Adam and Eve's eyes are opened, they see their nakedness, and cover up. But God created them as passionate sexual beings and called it all good. It's the desire for more and what that desire does to our capacity to judge between good and evil which may render our sexuality shameful.

There is such a tree at the centre of each of our lives. This tree bears fruit we should not go near if we are to have any kind of peace in our lives. For some it is booze, for others drugs. For some it's money. There are endless sources of addiction in a culture that spins the myth of insufficiency, like the serpent, and reminds us constantly we are not enough, we do not have enough, if something is good, then more is better. The serpent tells us we can handle it. We surely won't die. The serpent lies. If we reach out and grab this fruit, the god whose name is Just a Little More will demand absolute allegiance. What we think is good for us will turn out to be evil.

Our protagonist in *Le Bonheur* has everything. He just wants a little more. The abundance he has with his family is forgotten. His moral and ethical framework is hijacked in the service of his desire, and his capacity to know good from evil disappears. His moral reasoning becomes nothing more than self-serving justification for his desire. At this point, his fall is complete.

On a social level, the low-hanging fruit can be thought of as the extravagant, fossil-fuel and consumer-driven lifestyles at which we all grasp. The serpent whispers, "Did God say you couldn't enjoy any luxuries?" Well, no, not exactly. What God said was that if we don't put limits on our sense of entitlement, we're all going to die and take the planet with us. "Phooey," the serpent whispers, "you can have everything you want and more. Our capacity to judge between good and evil becomes skewed. We embrace what is ultimately destructive, as God warned us we would ("you will surely die"), and we turn away from what can save us.

Or, we could go to the political realm. Although our former Prime Minister would like nothing better than to trivialize the whole Gomery Inquiry, it strikes me that it's a tawdry story of bureaucrats, politicians, and business people whose eyes got fixated on some low-hanging fruit. They hear the serpent whisper: "you're entitled to skim a little off the top, here. After all, you're playing your part in saving a nation, so what's a couple hundred thousand here and there?" The cover-ups, the evasions of responsibility, the false indignation are symptoms of a tainted ethical and moral framework twisted to justify a desire for just a little more.

Who, then, will "clear the chaos and the clutter, and clear our eyes that we may see all the things that really matter, and help us to be at peace?" In this season of Lent, we are called to follow Jesus into the wilderness to sort this matter out. Jesus can't do it for us, but he can show us the way. He can show us that it's possible to resist the voice of the Satan within. You understand, I know, that "the serpent" and "the Satan" are mythological personifications of the forces within and without which tempt us out of our quiet centre.

We'd be mistaken if we assumed that the plate of fruit that Satan sets before Jesus was not tempting. In this story of his temptations, we get an inner glimpse into the spiritual struggle of Jesus as he is about to launch his ministry. What does Satan offer him? More power, more status, and more wealth. And if Jesus was looking for a way to rationalize taking this fruit, Satan helps him out by giving him the Scriptural warrant for each. Satan epitomizes the fall from grace in his unabashed use of the good for evil purposes.

With each temptation, Jesus chooses to collapse into the grace of what God has already provided. He is enough. He has enough. He chooses to love what he has been given, rather than to strive for more. He'll take the stones as they are and live off the bread of God's words. He'll take his peasant life and the people God has given him to love, and he'll discover more wealth there than all the silver and gold. He'll trust that he is God's beloved rather than create dramas to test God's love. He's found the frame in which he is free, and his freedom is now dedicated to the service of humanity.

Once the power of the desire for more holds no sway over Jesus, his quiet presence both comforts the afflicted and afflicts the comfortable. Demons fly from his presence. Religious teachers submit to his authority. Kings grow paranoid. Governors summon him to find out his secret. The sick flock to him for healing. People leave their livelihoods and their families to follow him. Beggars cry out to him. Insane demoniacs find themselves in their right minds. Corrupt tax collectors repent of their corruption. Soldiers try to scourge away his quiet centre. He forgives them. They mock him. He looks upon them with compassion. Powerful men crucify him. God raises him from the grave. Let us draw near to this risen, living Presence, as we commit, in this Lenten journey, to find our own way to the desert in search of a quiet centre.

—February 13, 2005

What God Wants

MICAH 6:1-8: MATTHEW 5:1-12

God has told you, mortals, what is good, and what does the Lord require of you, but to do justice, to love kindness, and to walk humbly with your God.

T he Hebrew God is not afraid to mix it up. The God of Greek philosophy, by comparison, is rather boring: omnipotent, unchanging, Pure Being. Yawn. But the Biblical God rolls up God's sleeves and dukes it out with the people. A good argument, for example, has half a chance of changing God's mind and course of action. Moses changes God's mind, as does Lot. Job had a harder time but at least he was given a hearing. In today's reading, God's people have gone way off track. God deals with this not by throwing lightning bolts from the sky, but rather by taking the people to court and making a case against them.

The prophet Micah imagines the Lord bringing a prophetic lawsuit against His people. Micah plays the role of presiding judge. He calls the court to order and then invites God to make God's case to the jury, which consists of the hills and the mountains. Creation is imbued with the authority and the wisdom to decide the case. One can only wonder how sympathetic creation would be to human beings of the 21st century. The people of God will be accused of going astray from an ancient covenant, with both creation and with the Creator.

The Lord then opens his case with a question, "O my people,

230

how have I wearied you? Answer me!" The people have become weary, and what follows makes it clear what has caused that weariness. The people have story-fatigue. They've forgotten the story which tells them where they came from, how they got to where they are, and how they're supposed to live. We know from the rest of Micah that the people are enjoying a rare period of prosperity, which is good. But what is not so good is that they're behaving badly. A short list of their bad behaviour includes coveting other people's fields and using their power to seize them; oppressing poor people, prophets, and priests; taking bribes, lying; and putting profit ahead of people.

God is baffled. He reminds them of their story. Don't you remember, God asks them, that you were once yourselves slaves in Egypt? Don't you remember that Pharaoh made slaves of all of you and how it feels to be nobodies? Don't you remember that in the interests of justice I set you free? So how, then, can you act unjustly toward the poor? How can you economically enslave others? Don't you remember your time in the wilderness when I sustained you? You neither starved nor died of thirst. You learned the meaning of sufficiency. So where did you learn about greed? When did you learn the mistrustfulness of which greed is a symptom? How can you now behave like the empires that have oppressed you? God concludes that they must have wearied of their sacred story, and without the story, they had lost their moorings.

There is a tiny island in the middle of the Indian Ocean. It is located in the direct path that last month's tsunami took. Seventy thousand people live on the island. Only seven were killed when the wave hit. When an islander was asked by a journalist why so few lost their lives, he replied that everyone on the island knows the story of the last tsunami which hit 100 years ago. Since then, every child in every generation has heard the story. The children are told that, when they feel the ground shake, they are to run to the hills in the centre of the island. The people of the island did not weary of their story. They knew that their people would live and die by that story.

It's no different for us. The reason we teach the Biblical story is simply that we know that once the church wearies of the Great Story, the church will perish. I'm not simply talking about this particular story or that story within the Bible, nor of picking our favourite Bible verses and memorizing them, though there's nothing wrong with memorizing Scripture. We need to learn the great sweep of the story, or we'll get fixated on details and then use them to support our favourite hobby horses.

Dr. James Dobson, who started Focus on the Family, is an evangelical preacher and child psychologist. He reaches 200 million people a week. Currently, he's using the Bible to warn people of the evils of gay marriage. His organization has now spread its influence to Canada in support of Mr. Harper, Leader of our Opposition. Doesn't it say in Genesis that a "man shall leave his father and mother and cleave to his wife?"

I can imagine God asking him and his followers "Have you wearied of the story?" There are many stories in the Bible, as I have said, but taken as a whole it is a counter-cultural narrative of God being with the victims of the dominant culture. The people who know what's it's like to be enslaved and oppressed by Empire don't need to be taught to be suspicious of the value systems of Empire. They know that Empire thought it was perfectly normal to enslave or treat as second class the stranger, the outsider, the person of different colour or sexual orientation.

Are there places in Scripture that speak against homosexuality? Sure, but not as many as you might be led to believe. But in this developing sacred narrative, the evolving consciousness of God's people, culminating for us in Jesus of Nazareth, the narrative thrust is toward greater inclusiveness, justice for the left-behinds of the world, and most importantly, toward a profound humility. This must include intellectual as well as spiritual humility. We don't claim that the story of our faith is Truth with a capital T. We claim that, by situating ourselves within a story that is told from the perspective of the victims of the dominant culture, we habitually ask ourselves whose interests are being served by this or that position. When we stop being suspicious of the pronouncements and predilections of a dominant culture, we have indeed "wearied of our story."

Germany was a Christian nation when Hitler came to power. Dietrich Bonhoeffer, a theologian and pastor, served in Germany during the rise of the Nazi Party. He wrote about the evils of nationalism. He challenged his fellow pastors. Were they wearying of the story of God's love for all people, the story of Jesus as humble servant, and adopting instead a narrative of power, embodied in the Nazi Party and incarnate in Hitler? He wrote that all it took for evil to flourish was for good people to remain silent. The Holocaust occurred with precious little protest from the church in Germany or from around the world. They had wearied of the Great Story that tells of what happens when people and nations refuse to live in covenant relationship with God: the void is filled by self-aggrandizement, nationalism, and the desire for absolute power which belongs to God alone. The cost of wearying of the sacred narrative was the death of millions of Jews, Romani, and gay and lesbian persons. It is right and good for the United Nations to help us to remember. Bonhoeffer was executed for his opposition to the Nazi Party. Blessed are those who are persecuted for righteousness' sake, indeed.

The present administration of United States of America is

experimenting with adopting a story of Empire and domination. Please understand, I am not comparing this current administration to Nazi Germany. I am in no danger of being imprisoned, for example, by speaking out in opposition to them. But those closest to the President are openly admitting imperial ambition to dominate the world. I will give them the benefit of the doubt and concede that they are doing this with the best of intentions. To them, this is the moment in history to use the unrivalled power of the US to impose on the rest of the world the ideals that they hold sacrosanct. Even if one optimistically trusts that those ideals are noble, the coercive means by which they are being pursued run counter to the Jesus story. Jesus proclaimed the Kingdom of God, for example but, unlike some of his contemporaries, refused the temptation to impose it by force. We celebrate today with the Iraqi people as they make their way to the polling stations for the first time in 50 years. But can freedom be imposed by outsiders? Time will tell. Rome's favourite slogan was *Pax Romana*, the peace of Rome. This peace came at the cost of first destroying nations, and then economically subjugating entire populations. History may prove my caution to be unwarranted. But I think the cost is already too high.

The story of imperial ambition is the oldest story known to humanity and many of us thought that, after the Cold War, there was an opportunity to retire it. This story is the persistent backdrop of the entire Biblical narrative. It is the story of Egypt, Babylon, Greece, and Rome. God's people developed their own narrative precisely in opposition to these powers, because these powers annihilated them repeatedly. This story of Empire is the backdrop of the Jesus story. The blessings we know as the Beatitudes were meant not for the Roman oppressors but for those who had felt the boot of Rome pressed firmly against their necks. Blessed are you who, in spite of this oppression, choose to live out your own sacred story with humility.

Even Republicans like Pat Buchanan are terrified of the path the neo-conservatives have taken. He reminds his readers in his latest book, *Where the Right Went Wrong*, that the US was founded on a story, not of Empire, but of resistance to the British Empire. The President may have his own personal Jesus, but has he wearied of the story of Jesus' courageous resistance to Empire? Has he wearied of the story of those early followers who were persecuted for righteousness' sake, those who were marginalized and executed because of their resistance to Empire? This witness of history and of the Bible is that all stories of Empire end as they began, in violence.

Joan Chittister, a Catholic nun, was in Ireland on the day President Bush was being sworn in for his second term. It was front-page news in North America. This story, Chittister notes, did not make the front page in Ireland. She said that throughout Europe, in fact, front pages were filled, not with the solemn ceremonies and sacred rituals of Empire but with an image of a young Iraqi girl, covered with the blood of her parents. In the car from which she has been pulled, her mother's and father's bodies are riddled with bullets. Their family was going on a vacation and they didn't see the soldiers telling them to stop their car.

When the people have forgotten their story, sacred rituals become empty, meaningless, and ultimately grotesque. It doesn't impress God how many times you lift your arms up and praise Jesus, when children are being traumatized and killed in the name of freedom. God stands before the mountains and hills and continues his case against those who have wearied of the sacred story. "With what shall I come before the Lord and bow myself before God on high?" God asks, assuming the voice of the people. God then recites a litany of escalating violence, burnt offerings, year-old calves, thousands of rams. This frenzy of violent sacrifice ends with the most abhorrent practice of all to God, human sacrifice, the offering of first-born children. The amnesia is absolute when the people begin to believe that it is necessary to sacrifice children for their sacred cause.

Is this the sacrifice God requires? The prophet steps in to answer God's questions to the people. "God has told you, o mortals, what is good; and what does the Lord require of you, but to do justice, love kindness, and to walk humbly with your God."

In the end, the Biblical narrative is a story of humility that exposes and undermines the story of Empire; it culminates in the story of a God who emptied God's self of all power and dwelled with the people in Jesus Christ. It tells the story of Jesus Christ, who further emptied himself of power and died on a cross so that we might know some way other way to be together than through the exercise of violence. In the Beatitudes, he confers his blessing upon those who do not weary of the story but rather embrace it at great personal cost. We tell this sacred story to our children, we retell it to ourselves, day after day, because it is, in the end, a story of life and death. We tell it because, when the ground beneath us begins to shake, we will know where to go to find refuge.

—January 30, 2005

Binners, the Baby Jesus, and Us

LUKE 2:1-20

In that region there were shepherds living in the fields, keeping watch over their flock by night.

In a recent article in the *Vancouver Sun*, Douglas Todd wrote a story about a modern-day saint, Ken Lyotier, who has started a business in the downtown Eastside called "United We Can." A former Eastside binner, Ken now employs a host of those people who push grocery carts down our back lanes looking for recyclable bottles and other refuse that may bring them a couple of bucks. One of our ministers has gotten to know a few of these local folks. She invites them to come to worship, but they're too self-conscious. They don't say it in so many words, but when one of them assured her that if he ever did show up he'd make sure that he had a shower before he came, she caught his drift.

If you had to rewrite the Christmas script today, we'd probably cast Mr. Lyotier as an angel, but he wouldn't stand for it. "Being a Christian," he told Todd, "is being a friend to these people." That kind of simplifies things, doesn't it? Reverend Killian Noe agrees. Her ministry is to the addicted folk in downtown Seattle. She's really working on getting past metaphors of "serving" the poor; her church befriends them.

No, if Mr. Lyotier were to accept any role in the holy pageant of Christmas Eve, I suspect he might choose to represent the shepherds. They were the despised of Jesus' day. "You could smell them before you ever saw them" is what the local people said about shepherds, the same way we might say that you can hear the rattle of the binners' homes on wheels before you ever see them. Our back lanes are the modern-day equivalent of the Bethlehem hills that the shepherds called home.

Interesting, isn't it, that it was these very hills where the heavenly host made their appearance that first Christmas? That God chose to announce the holy birth through shepherds should give us pause. When the angel of the Lord stood before them and said, "do not be afraid; for see, I am bringing good news of great joy for all the people," the word in that proclamation which would have rung in their ears like a Christmas bell, was "all." If they weren't so gobsmacked by angels coming to them rather than to the good townspeople, they might have sought clarification: "Now, Mr. Angel of the Lord, when you say 'all the people' who exactly did you have in mind?"

Ken Lyotier shared with Douglas Todd that he himself had been on the receiving end of hilltop religious experiences during his active binner days. He didn't call them angelic visitations, but perhaps on Christmas Eve, he might allow us some literary licence. Whatever you call them, they changed his life. One time, it happened in a church. He just felt moved to get up and preach a message of social justice, of God coming to the dumpster brigade with good news. They called the cops, as any respectable church might, perhaps because they thought he was high and perhaps he was; but I wonder if, in hindsight, that congregation wonders if they were visited unawares by a heavenly messenger, a message of great joy for "all the people." It was disruptive, I'm sure, but then again, this Christmas message is nothing if not disruptive.

So God takes on human flesh and dwells among us to proclaim good news to the poor? It makes sense when you stop to think about it. I received an email to the effect that, if you've got food in the fridge and a roof over your head, you are richer than 75% of the world. If you have a little money in the bank, a wallet with a few bills in it, and spare change in a dish somewhere in the house, you are among the top 8% of the world's wealthy. It shouldn't surprise us too much today either, that when the angels were sent on that first Christmas mission, all of their visitations were first to the poor. Majority rules. Most human beings were poor then, as most are now on this planet earth.

This doesn't mean God loves my local bottle collector, Harry, any more than God loves you or me. The blessing of this birth is meant for all the people. God knows impoverishment is as much a spiritual matter as it is a material one. My hunch is that our core impoverishment as affluent people is that we don't know God, not really. We've also realized in our more honest moments that no amount of stuff, and no bank account no matter what size, can fill the emptiness of not knowing the One who made us.

We're all out there rattling down the back lane of our lives, desperately filling our shopping carts with one thing or another, with excitement, with the next relationship, with alcohol and prescription drugs, whatever it takes to fend off the gnawing restlessness that is our soul's longing to return to God. In the code language of the Christmas story, this return home is called the journey to Bethlehem. We arrive tonight for the tradition of it; certainly, to sing the carols, absolutely; to be with family—you bet. But we arrive here at the stable door tonight as well, drawn by the mysterious longing to know God.

Here we are at the stable, all of us, the Henrys, Mr. Lyotier, the rich and the poor, the penniless shepherds and the gift-laden wise men. We gather around the Christ child who is, we're told, God with us. This is the one who reveals to us the God our soul longs to know. The moment we make a place in our heart for the child, we will realize that this yearning which unites us is stronger than whatever we imagine separates us. As Christ grows in our hearts, we grow in our desire to befriend the outcast; we may find ourselves asking our own back-lane binners if they have a name; that's the disruptive part—the holy peace which the multitude of heavenly hosts proclaimed to the shepherds. That is also the hopeful part, perhaps a first small step we can all take toward peace on earth, in this city, in our own back lanes.

—December 24, 2004

Beyond Fear

GENESIS 37:1-4, 12-28; MATTHEW 14:22-23

*So Peter got out of the boat, started walking on the
water and came toward Jesus. But when he noticed a
strong wind, he became frightened, and beginning to
sink, he cried out… "save me."*

Peter just about pulls it off. He sees Jesus walking on water
and thought he just might be able to bring it off himself. It's
fear that causes him to plunge into the stormy waters. At the root
of their envy and jealousy it was fear as well that caused Joseph's
brothers to plot his demise. One of the spiritual disciplines I have
long wanted to engage in is the careful tracking of fear in my life
and its effect on my decisions and my way of being in the world.
This may seem a strange spiritual discipline to be attracted to, but
I am convinced that fear has a much greater influence in our lives,
both privately and collectively, than we care to admit.

The other night, around 1:30, as we were sleeping, I heard
someone walk briskly by our bedroom windows and down the
small alleyway that leads to our back patio. I sat up quietly, as I did
not want to alarm Ann or draw the attention of our intruder. I
slipped on my dressing gown and tiptoed upstairs to inspect. My
heart was pounding, the adrenalin coursing through my veins.
Sure enough, I could see through the kitchen window a small
flashlight checking things out on the patio. I retreated hastily
down the stairs and called the police. Whoever it was got away, but

I can tell you it was a restless night. I've never understood people's attraction to scary movies. I do not understand people deliberately choosing to feel the way I felt that night. I guess it is a rush of sorts, but you have to be desperate for excitement to do this to yourself. Personally, I'd rather sleep at night.

This is one kind of fear, an external force that threatens our security. But the more subtle and perhaps more determinative fears come from within, precisely because they often operate unconsciously. It's the more subtle forms of fear that interest me. Karl Barth wrote: "Fear is the anticipation of a supposedly certain defeat." I'm interested in the fear that signals to us that a future decidedly not of our choosing is fixed and certain, that we're going to suffer some kind of defeat, emotionally, psychologically, relationally. It is this certainty of defeat that often becomes a self-fulfilling prophecy. Our worst fears are realized.

Pete Sampras, perhaps the greatest tennis player of all time, has been free-falling in the ratings in the past couple of years. His biggest problem, he will tell you, is that he's lost confidence. Whereas once he just knew he could hit a backhand winner down the line, now he's thinking twice about the shot. All that stands between the true champion and the rest of the field is this split second, in which you either know you're going to make the shot or you have that nanosecond of fear that prevents you from committing to it. Fear is Pete's most formidable opponent at this time in his career.

Jesus has broken open the boundaries of what just might be possible. With a little encouragement Peter overcomes his fears, and like a little child taking the first few steps, he's doing it! Then he notices the wind and the waves and what he's doing that he is not supposed to be able to do. Fear enters, and the moment he anticipates defeat, it's over.

It's a bit staggering to keep track of the number of times fear affects us on a daily basis; I'm talking about little explosions of fear that pass so quickly through our consciousness as thoughts and images that we barely notice. Here's my own partial fear list that I compete with on a daily basis. I'm afraid of getting something wrong, of saying the wrong thing, of being at a party I'm not invited to. I'm afraid of too much power and too much success, because then people start expecting too much of me. I'm afraid of too little power and success, because then I won't have any influence. I'm afraid of forgetting the words to a song in the middle of a performance. I'm afraid that my voice is not good enough to be singing in public. I'm afraid of being poor. I'm afraid I'm boring, of what you think about me. I'm afraid I'll wake up one morning and have no faith. I'm afraid the born-again Christians are right and I'm wrong. I'm afraid of opening my heart. I'm afraid I'll make an error in judgment when I'm counseling someone, of losing my memory, of my body going flabby. I'm afraid I'll run out of things to say once and for all on a Sunday morning. I'm afraid of dying, particularly by drowning. I'm afraid that Ann will fall and break another bone. These are the fears of a relatively well-adjusted person, and they are always lurking just beneath the surface of my awareness. Who will save us?

The story of Joseph's brothers selling him into slavery in Egypt is an interesting one on a number of different levels, but I want to focus on the brothers' fears as a motivating factor in their decision. Joseph is the favoured brother. His father, Jacob, whom we met last week, has made him a special coat of many colours, which seriously annoys his brothers. On top of this, Joseph has unwisely chosen to share a couple of dreams, which serves to reinforce his special status in the Universe. But what really galls them is hearing that what they essentially mean is that Joseph will rule over them. What is surprising in the story is the depth of their expression of anger. They are ready to kill him. They hate Joseph. If it seems a little extreme, my hunch is that what they are dealing with at core is fear. C.S. Lewis has written: "hatred is often the compensation by which a frightened man reimburses himself for the miseries of Fear...the stronger the fear the more intense the hatred." What they may fear is that the dreams are true. In the either/or consciousness of the male psyche; if Joseph is special, then perhaps they are not. If Joseph is specially loved by their father, then maybe they are not. If Joseph indeed has been chosen by God, then perhaps they have been forgotten. It's fear that hatches their violent plot.

We often turn fear into hatred because we're unconscious of the fear. This is especially true of men, who have been socialized away from fear. It is an unacceptable feeling, so it gets expressed as anger and even hatred. A simple example: 20 years or so ago, I was driving to Barrie, Ontario en route to my ordination service. My mom and dad were in the back seat, and Ann was in the front seat. I was driving down the Don Valley Parkway at 120 clicks, and someone cut me off. Well, I let loose some expletives which would curl your toenails, and after I settled down, I remembered I had some backseat passengers, who up to this point were pretty proud of their son. It was fear, not anger, which issued in the expletives. Road rage is about men compensating for fear with anger and hatred because they cannot admit being frightened. Are wars started and sustained because men are unwilling to tell each other that they are frightened, so the fear gets expressed as hatred and rage?

Fear of not being loved prevents us from being our genuine selves, doesn't it? Alice Miller wrote a bestseller called *The Drama of the Gifted Child*. The title is not really reflective of the book. She is a psychologist who was one of the first to recognize the extent to which we go, as children, to procure the love of our parents when we are afraid it is not given unconditionally. We learn to be charming, to be good little boys and girls, to withhold unpleasant feelings, to excel to the extent that we fashion, out of fear of not being loved, a self which aims to please others but is alien to our genuine self. This self Alice Miller called the false self. From my observations, if we have not gone through an intentional process of discovering our own unique false self, we will carry this inauthentic self into our adulthood. The symptoms are depression, anxiety, and a distinct lack of spontaneity, for fear of doing something or saying something that might displease someone, somewhere. It's fear that keeps us operating from a false self in the world.

Okay then, what do we do about fear and how does the Christian faith help? Jesus is often presented in mainstream Christianity as the one who saves us from sin. From this framework, the central problem of the human condition is sin. But in this story, Peter cries out to Jesus to save him, not from sin but from the effects of fear. Jesus dealt with sin by forgiving it, but fear is more challenging.

Jesus is the one who saves us from fear, not by taking it away from us but rather by inviting us to enter more deeply into our fears. There's an expression that says: "The way out is the way in." Jesus validates Peter's courageous gesture by helping him to lean into his fear and go for it. He doesn't take it away, but he makes it clear that, with more faith, he could overcome his fear and go beyond the limits of what he thought possible.

In the gospels, Jesus is portrayed as one who is more powerful than the elements, including elemental fears. He is the embodiment of the One who at creation spoke into the watery chaos and darkness and called for life. He is Lord of all, and therefore Lord over fear itself. We make a claim that this power to overcome fear in our life is available for the asking if we will open our hearts and allow Christ to enter. When Christ is Lord, or Sovereign in our lives, the chaos created by fear is calmed and the story of creation becomes our personal story. The voice that spoke at the beginning of creation speaks into our debilitating fears and, like Peter, we are encouraged to step into our fears and conquer them, with the power of Christ at our disposal. It's not so important that Peter's successful overcoming of his fear was short-lived. He got wet. So what? The important thing is that Jesus was there to pull him out, and reassure him that this was just the beginning of a new life not controlled by fear.

When the disciples realize the power of Jesus, the story says that they began to worship him. There are two kinds of fear in the Bible. There's the kind I've been discussing, which we all know too well. But there's also the "fear of God," which should be translated "awe." This is a fundamental spiritual transformation, when debilitating fear is replaced by awe. It signals that we have finally got it. Awe is born of the awareness that there really is a Presence more powerful than fear. It goes by the name of love, and it does cast out fear. It frees us to be our most authentic selves, to speak prophetic truth to powers which rule through fear, to go beyond the limits which fear imposes, so that we can step out into the life God intends for us. In Christ there is a life beyond fear. It is our divine inheritance. Let us claim it as our own in the name of this awesome Christ.

—August 11, 2002

Movement of the Spirit

I CORINTHIANS 12:1-11

To each is given the manifestation of the
Spirit for the common good.

What's a life for? The question is not new in my life. But it's been muscling its way into my consciousness with a little more persistence recently. It could just be a mid-life thing. I've got fewer years left on this planet than I've put in so far. I'm over the hump, but what's left for me to do before I'm over the hill? The good news is that I know there are many in this congregation in their late 80s and beyond who are still on the upward ascent, so there's still time to respond to the question. One of my favourite songwriters, Bruce Cockburn, sings a line: "I've got this thing in my heart I must give you today; it only lives when you give it away."

Something's brewing within me. Certain triggers seem to bring it to life. On Friday night, a bunch of us went to see *The Corporation*, a new documentary playing at the Ridge Theatre this week. One of the stories told took place in Bolivia, a desperate nation that turned to the World Bank and the International Monetary Fund for assistance. As a condition of receiving financial assistance, the country was required to privatize their public companies. They were required, for example, to privatize the water supply. A foreign company took the job. The local people were fined for gathering rainwater. It was now considered the private property of the company. The people took to the streets, and they took back their water. As I watched the people rise up, this "thing" inside of me, this nascent life, stirred. This life, I realize, desires to be given away in the service of something like that. There were 1,200 people in the theatre and my hunch is that I wasn't alone. You could feel it.

I want to be part of a movement that makes a difference in the direction of a more just, peaceful and sustainable world. Now this is a bit scary for a middle-class, white, North American male who enjoys the attendant privileges and luxuries of this particular demographic. This "thing in my heart" may be calling me to give up my attachments to such privileges.

I shouldn't really be so surprised by the emergence of this desire. After all I'm already part of a movement. It's called the church. Originally it wasn't called "church." It was a movement of ordinary people who became known as "people of the way," which is a much more dynamic image than "church." Ordinary people were activated by Jesus of Nazareth, who helped them understand that God's vision of a just and humane world was distinctly different from Caesar's vision. For one thing, God's vision embraced all of humanity and all of creation, not just the élite. Jesus did nothing more or less than to ask the powers if they weren't forgetting something, namely 90% of the population. He also pointed out to the people that they might be forgetting something as well, that they had more power than they might think. Those who followed Jesus of Nazareth to his death and beyond his death realized that God in Christ had initiated a movement of justice and peace.

I've been thinking lately about the potential of this movement called the church. In order for the potential to be realized as a servant of cultural and political transformation, however, we need to shed an image of the church we may have grown up with. It's difficult not to think of the church more as a destination than as a movement; in this view, church is a static place we all go to for various reasons, for inspiration, guidance, and meaning, in order to fill ourselves up and return to our everyday lives. This is not a bad thing, as far as it goes, but what if the inspiration, guidance, and meaning are not ends in themselves but rather means to an end, which historically the church has called mission? It's this component which transforms a congregation from being a spiritual gas station at which we fill our tanks on a weekly basis, to a movement, the purpose of which is to fuel up and fan out, and by the power of the Holy Spirit to comfort those who mourn, to heal the sick, to clothe the naked and feed the hungry, and speak truth to power. You see, that's a movement, and when the church starts to see itself as a movement, then the Holy Spirit's got something to work with.

The Holy Spirit was moving all over and through the early church in ways that make good United Church people squirm a little. It was the norm for those who had made a decision to follow Christ to receive a spiritual booster shot. These came in the form of gifts. Some of these gifts Paul himself had reservations about, like speaking in tongues. Paul didn't question that people got caught up in this kind of ecstatic gibberish, but basically he relegated it to a very minor gift. But the other gifts, like faith, administration, knowledge, discernment of spirits, and healing, he took very seriously. He describes them as "manifestations of the Spirit for the common good." At Canadian Memorial, we're taking these gifts seriously. We have a process anyone can go through to discover the gifts God has given him or her to be used in the service of the common good. These gifts did not confer special status; having one and not another did not mean one was more privileged in God's eyes; and more importantly they were not for personal growth or private titillation. They were for the "common good." This thing in my heart, the same thing that's in your heart, may just be the particular gift God has given you to be used in the service of the common good. This is what we're called to give away, if we want the divine life in us to flourish.

We're living through perhaps the most narcissistic era in the history of humanity. Increasingly, we understand ourselves as private citizens with private rights to pursue our private interests. Our responsibility in this culture is to consume. We are fuel for the economic system. It is this economic system that is sovereign today. The so-called "invisible hand of the market" is given free rein. Any attempt by government to point it in the direction of the common good is legislated against. There are clauses in all free trade agreements stipulating that if a nation acts in the interests of the common good, it can be sued.

You watch a movie like *The Corporation* and you come away realizing just how radical an idea the common good is today. The modern-day corporations are the high priests of our culture, touching, influencing, and controlling every aspect of our lives. We have become servants of corporations, with little time or energy left over for pursuit of the common good. In the singular pursuit of profit, the film makes a compelling case that corporations manifest every character of the psychopathic personality disorder: inability to sustain meaningful relationships, disregard for the law, the inability to feel or express guilt, and a heightened capacity for deceit. Now this is a bit unfair, I know. Many of us work for corporations that make good products, are run by good people, and give back to society in the form of charitable gifts. So it is not helpful to demonize corporations or their leaders.

But one of the gifts of the Spirit is the discernment of spirits.

We're called as followers of Jesus to discern when and where fundamental allegiance has shifted away from God and towards other powers, and to name this shift. Theologically, we affirm that all powers, including corporations, are good; they are created by God. But all powers, like all people, have fallen, by which I mean that fundamental desires have reversed course, away from the common good for which they were created and back toward private interests. Finally, all powers, including corporate culture, can be redeemed and return to the household of God. The Greek word for household, incidentally, is *oikonomos*, translated also as economy.

One of the most hopeful interviews in the documentary was with Ray Anderson, CEO of Interface, one of the largest commercial carpet corporations in the world. He shares how his customers began to ask him about his company's ecological vision. He didn't have one, but a group of employees organized a conference of their worldwide plants and asked him to give the opening speech. He scrambled to get some material and came across a book called *Ecology and Commerce*, a damming indictment of the corporate world's plundering of the earth. He speaks of a spear piercing his heart as he was convicted of wrongdoing. In fact, he became certain that one day people would be arrested for what he had done to the earth. Then a clip is shown of Mr. Anderson addressing a gathering of his colleagues in industry. He begins with the words, "Do I know you all well enough to address you as fellow plunderers of the earth?" His company has a vision of zero footprint by the year 2020.

It doesn't matter if Ray Anderson is a Christian or not. The Spirit is not limited to churches, thank goodness. His is a description of redemption, of God-given desires reversing course and flowing toward the common good. The lance which pierced his heart was no less a manifestation of the Holy Spirit for the common good because it took place within his corporation. In fact, isn't it possible that the next great movement of the Holy Spirit will occur through the employees of corporations, who have this "thing in their heart" that they must give away so that it can live, so that all creatures can live and thrive upon this miracle of life called the planet earth? God has given each of us gifts, which are manifestations of Spirit. When we decide collectively to set them loose in the world, we have a movement, a movement of Spirit. It just may be that *this* is what our lives are for.

—*January 18, 2004*